ne

Wild

Side

7/94

OTHER WORKS BY NICHOLAS CHRISTOPHER

Poetry

On Tour with Rita *(1982)*
A Short History of the Island of Butterflies *(1986)*
Desperate Characters: A Novella in Verse & Other Poems *(1988)*
In the Year of the Comet *(1992)*
5° & Other Poems *(1995)*

Fiction

The Soloist *(1986)*

Anthologies

Under 35: The New Generation of American Poets *(1989)*

Walk on the Wild Side

URBAN AMERICAN POETRY
SINCE 1975

Edited by Nicholas Christopher

Collier Books
Macmillan Publishing Company • New York
Maxwell Macmillan Canada • Toronto
Maxwell Macmillan International
New York • Oxford • Singapore • Sydney

Collier Books   Maxwell Macmillan Canada, Inc.
Macmillan Publishing Company   1200 Eglinton Avenue East,
866 Third Avenue   Suite 200
New York, NY 10022   Don Mills, Ontario M3C 3N1

Macmillan Publishing Company is part of the Maxwell Communication
Group of Companies.

Library of Congress Cataloging-in-Publication Data
Walk on the wild side : urban American poetry since 1975 / edited by
    Nicholas Christopher.
        p.   cm.
    ISBN 0-02-042725-5 (pbk.)—ISBN 0-684-19623-9
    1. American poetry—20th century—History and criticism.   2. City
    and town life in literature.   3. Cities and towns in literature.
    I. Christopher, Nicholas.
    PS310.C58W35   1993   93-29443   CIP
    811'.54091732—dc20

Macmillan books are available at special discounts for bulk purchases for
sales promotions, premiums, fund-raising, or educational use. For details,
contact:

Special Sales Director
Macmillan Publishing Company
866 Third Avenue
New York, NY 10022

Book Design by Ellen R. Sasahara

10 9 8 7 6 5 4 3 2 1

Printed in the United States of America

Contents

About the Editor

Nicholas Christopher was born in 1951, and was graduated from Harvard College. He is the author of five books of poems: *On Tour with Rita* (Knopf, 1982), *A Short History of the Island of Butterflies* (Viking, 1986), *Desperate Characters: A Novella in Verse & Other Poems* (Viking, 1988), *In the Year of the Comet* (Viking, 1992), and *5° & Other Poems* (Viking, 1994). He has published a novel, *The Soloist* (Viking, 1986), and he edited the anthology *Under 35: The New Generation of American Poets* (Anchor, 1989). His book about film noir and the American city, *Somewhere in the Night,* is forthcoming from The Free Press. He is the recipient of numerous awards, including Poetry Fellowships from the National Endowment for the Arts and the New York Foundation for the Arts, the Amy Lowell Poetry Travelling Fellowship, and the Peter I. B. Lavan Award from The Academy of American Poets. Most recently, he was awarded a Guggenheim Fellowship in Poetry for 1993–94. He has published his work widely in leading magazines and literary journals and in various anthologies in the United States and abroad, and has taught at several universities, including Yale, Barnard College, Columbia, and New York University. He lives in New York City.

Introduction

Unlike the countries of Europe, not to mention Japan and China, the United States boasts enormous cities today, at the end of the so-called "American Century," that barely existed one hundred fifty years ago. Los Angeles is a good example: a mission settlement belonging to Spain in 1830, by 1945 it had become a five-thousand-square-mile sprawl. In 1830, Detroit was a trading post on a dirt crossroads. Houston a muddy frontier town called Harrisburg. San Francisco a small hilltop settlement that went by the name Yerba Buena. Chicago had yet to be incorporated as a village. Denver and Seattle, of course, didn't even exist. In historical terms, our urban culture has developed at hothouse speed, with all attendant hothouse permutations and outgrowths—spectacular, freakish, stunted, and delirious. Gilded ages worthy of Imperial Rome and slums to rival Calcutta's. Quicksilver migrations, immigrations, and displacements. Boom times and fierce depressions, in which whole industries, ethnic groups, and cultural phenomena have thrived and vanished in the wink of an eye.

All this in one hundred fifty years—hardly a blip on the screen of world history. With the Industrial Revolution, most of our big cities expanded exponentially after the Civil War. And from Whitman and Poe, our first truly urban poets (who took different forks off the same road), and then Stephen Crane to Hart Crane, there is a long and important line of poets that first becomes apparent with the consolidation of these cities as mass centers and continues to thrive in the present day megalopolis. If American rural poetry reflects the flux of nature, and of man-in-nature as both observer and participant, American urban poetry must mirror a far more complex sort of flux: not just of populations in a man-made environment, but of the myriad human activities and crosscurrents—economic, political, religious, sexual, intellectual, artistic—that define that environment. The tableau of urban poetry is, quite simply, all of human society and every occurrence therein—from the erection of skyscrapers and suspension bridges, to the game a child might invent on a sidewalk, to the words murmured between two mourners at a funeral. A literally infinite range of subject matter.

American cities are physical labyrinths, and also spiritual and metaphysical ones. The business of the city poet is to chronicle, explore, excavate, and reflect the byways, recesses, and inner chambers of that labyrinth. Sometimes the reflections he or she comes upon in the depths of the maze will be from a dark mirror, or a mirror of dizzying clarity, or even a funhouse mirror of strange distortions, but I would argue that the resultant poems represent the most vivid and significant strain in modern American poetry.

I should make clear that by "urban poetry" in this book's subtitle I do not only mean poems "about" cities, or poems with the city (generically or metaphysically) as a subject. Of course there are such poems in this book, but in choosing them, and the many other various poems I settled upon, I did not want to be restricted by such a narrow (and arbitrary) overall definition. As a starting point, I tried always to keep in mind the innumerable themes that the city (whatever American city it might be) would filter and radiate through its poets, and their poems, to their audience. How the basic themes of love, sex, renewal, memory, and death are dealt with from an urban perspective, in urban settings. A riveting city poem can be about a love affair, a dream, a meal, a midnight walk, a snowstorm, a crime; its perspective will be dictated by the imagination of the poet. In this book, the very particular lens for that perspective is the American city of our own time. The sort of city that contains, and is defined by, so many extremes: opulence and poverty, exhilarating beauty and harsh ugliness, private anonymity and public nakedness, salvation and corruption, mundane drugdery and spiritual transcendence, and so on. In short, I would hope that the poems in this anthology provide not just a unique overview of the astonishing and tumultuous events that have unfolded (or exploded) in American cities in recent years, but also a fresh and vibrant glimpse into the more private dramas and comedies of individual lives in metropolitan settings. For what is the poet in essence—however broad his cultural canvas—if not a spokesman for the individual (with all the *weight* that word carries, and should carry, for an American).

Emerson put it simply: "The poet has a new thought; he has a whole new experience to unfold; he will tell us how it was with him, and all men will be the richer in his fortune." In other words, in poetic terms, we might turn around the national motto, *E pluribus unum,* and proclaim instead, "From the one, many." Worlds unto themselves, our cities were fed during and after Reconstruction with crucially important migrants from the rural South— African-Americans, former slaves and the offspring of slaves—who, despite disenfranchisement on a grand scale, persecution legal and otherwise, and an obscene denial of basic human rights, intensified, enriched, and transformed our urban culture inestimably. At the same time in our history, there was a vast influx of immigrants, coming from every other country on the planet and flooding our cities. People with different languages, customs, beliefs—and prejudices. How much more complex, fertile, and volatile this has made our cities—in comparison to foreign cities like Tokyo whose national governments practically prohibit immigration of any kind, much less racial variety—cannot really be calculated. (Census takers in 1990 reported that a single four-square-block area in Queens, New York, boasted no less than one hundred eighteen different nationalities of registered aliens and foreign-born citizens!)

The German historian Oswald Spengler, writing on the eve of the First World War (when legal immigration to the United States was at its peak), stated that the emergence of New York as a "world-city" was the single most important development in the nineteenth century. It marked not only the ascendancy of the United States as the preeminent international power, but was also the historical moment in which American cities became the magnet for mass immigration. These immigrants and their successors, from Europe, Asia, Africa, and Latin America, literally built the American cities that we live in today, and the railroads and highways that connect them, as well as the wildly variegated (ever-expanding) cultural perimeters that give them their soul. A handful of those immigrants, and a somewhat larger handful of their offspring, have made the latter category of construction work—in the arts—their life's work. Poets speak for themselves, not for groups of people *per se*, but it is hoped that Americans of every stripe will find some familiar and comforting, or discordant and equally familiar, echo of their own voices in the words of the contributors to this book.

A word about the date in my subtitle, 1975, which also should be carefully explained. For the poems herein to be vitally "contemporary" (that is, to speak to us with some urgency), I did not envision as their tableau the whole of post–Second World War America, or even the America of the 1960's (which are not so close anymore, in poetic terms), but the America of the post-Vietnam, post-Watergate era—that is, after 1975. As we approach the end not just of the century but of the millennium, 1975, too, seems far off in time. In urban terms, it certainly is. One need only consider that two words with instant recognition in any American city today—"AIDS" and "crack"—were literally unknown anywhere two decades ago. In 1968, seventy-one percent of the people in the United States lived in cities, on one percent of the land. Today, over eighty-five percent of the population are city dwellers. And the last twenty years have marked an especially important period in the history of urban American poetry. If city life has gotten more intense on a day-to-day level, its poetry has certainly followed suit. Nineteen sixty-five marked the beginning of a cultural revolution in this country. In rock music. Drugs, from marijuana to psychedelics. Sexual mores. Patterns of marriage and divorce. While the U.S. government waged a bloody, unpopular, and futile war—the first war on foreign soil we would ever lose—citizens in legion numbers took to the streets at home to protest with fervor. They also joined marches for civil rights and women's rights, and rallied for numerous other social changes. The society was in ferment, and the arts were not only a part of that ferment, but also brought much of it about. And much of it, of course, was centered in the cities.

But if 1965 was the watershed year, 1975 marked both the end of that era and the beginning of a new one. Some would argue that it was a passive era, culminating in the reactionary and piously puritanical ethos (as well as the scandals and mendacity) of the

Reagan-Bush years. A period of retreat, of people taking stock—or taking flight. But for American poetry, 1975 marked the beginning of a renaissance that continues and flourishes to this day. Good poetry is not journalism—a set of narrowly topical, easy-to-digest "bulletins from the front." One can write a pamphlet in the heat of battle; it's tougher to write a good poem under such conditions, much less one that will endure beyond its own era and grow in power and relevance. Poets need to digest events big and small, inside and outside their own lives, and to be able to transform and distill them imaginatively with objectivity and detachment—with the "cold eye" that Yeats insisted was necessary for true poetic production. American poetry seemed to explode onto the page after 1975—not just because of its content and style, but because of the new generation of American poets who came of age with full heads and full hearts (spleens, too, on occasion) in the succeeding years. There was a hiatus of ten years between the social and cultural cataclysm that occurred in 1965 and the revolution in poetry that followed.

So the poets in this book, many shaped by the 1960's as children or young adults, left behind that oft-maligned, oft-celebrated decade by writing about it, its aftereffects, and most importantly, the countless new roads it opened up in American urban culture. Going down an uncharted river, one inevitably finds other uncharted rivers feeding into it and branching off it, and that seems to me roughly analagous to the experience of the contemporary American poet. If the 1960's were truly that first, complicated, never-quite-plumbed river, all succeeding years have been its often more fascinating, more aggressively navigated, tributaries. Frankly, there is no other period in this century that has produced more—and better—city poems by such an incredible variety of voices as the years since 1975.

Who are these voices and how did I go about collecting them? First, any book of this sort is by definition incomplete, and any poet in my position, editing such a book, can only assure the reader that every pain was taken, every bit of effort that time and budget allowed, to make the book as complete and comprehensive as possible. If some particular favorite of the reader's has been omitted, it is not due to lack of openmindedness, but to the sheer volume of very fine poetry I had to choose from and to the limitations of space that were imposed by necessity. Every anthology is as subjective an undertaking in the end as a writer's own novel or poetry collection, and any editor who claims otherwise is being disingenuous, at best. The ephemeral, frozen moment in which these sixty poets form a whole—this book—must create a complicated, often rebellious ratio between their many, multifarious poetic visions and my overall, necessarily imperfect, vision as editor. The inherent tension therein should be a stimulus to the reader, whether he agrees with every choice, every poem, or invariably, does not.

I tried to find poets writing in and about as many American cities as I could. Writing about them, not incidentally but with authority. In contemplating how I would structure the book, I rejected the notion of breaking it up by regions, or by the biggest cities—"Detroit," "Miami," "Los Angeles," etc. These might have been neat pigeonholes, but the poems coming out of Tulsa, Santa Fe, Honolulu, Baton Rouge, and Memphis that so enrich these pages would have been sorely missed, to say the least. So the poets are listed alphabetically—no gimmicks—and the cities, from all over the map, are to be found in their poems, not in chapter headings. I chose the poets with three criteria in mind: that they be American; that their poems be specifically rooted in American cities (no expatriate Paris or Tangier poems); and that their writing be of the highest quality—poems constructed with charged, inventive, and musical language. And with unique and powerful voices behind them.

I will let the variety of these voices speak for itself. For voices as diverse as those one might hear in a crowd, a schoolyard, a restaurant, or a stadium in any American city are what I want the reader to hear in these pages. Their styles run the gamut from surrealism and rap to neorealism and visionary narrative, from bare-bones street poetry to elegant dramatic monologues and ironic reveries.

Upon returning home to New York City in September 1870, after a long absence, Walt Whitman in *Democratic Vistas* gives us a loving testament of how the city provided him with as much, if not more, poetic fodder as "Nature . . . great in her fields of freedom and the open air." He compares the city's bright and dark sides: "the splendor, picturesqueness, and oceanic amplitude and rush of these great cities . . . the costly and lofty new buildings, facades of marble and iron . . . the heavy, low, musical roar, hardly ever intermitted, even at night." And this is also the city, he went on, that is "crowded with petty grotesques, malformations, phantoms," in which, everywhere, "in shop, street, church, theatre, bar-room, official chair, are pervading flippancy and vulgarity, low cunning, infidelity. . . ."

Of course today, as over a century ago, all our cities are both of these cities—and then some. The best of our urban poets deal with the bright and the dark, and the many more difficult, intricate, and ambiguous shades of nuance and purpose in between. Whitman, ever torn, insisted he took heart from the redemptive possibilities and sheer vitality of the city's "ingenuities, streets, goods, houses . . . these electric crowds of men." I hope that the reader will find not only a good deal of heart and hard-earned wisdom and crucial intelligence in the following pages, but also plenty of electricity as well.

—Nicholas Christopher
New York City, February 1994

For their generous assistance and support at the various stages of this book's evolution, I am grateful to my editors at Scribners, Charles Flowers and Hamilton Cain, to my agent, Anne Sibbald, and to my wife, Constance Christopher.

Walk on the Wild Side

The Good Shepherd: Atlanta, 1981

I lift the boy's body
from the trunk,
set it down,
then push it over the embankment
with my foot.
I watch it roll
down into the river
and feel I'm rolling with it,
feel the first cold slap of the water,
wheeze and fall down on one knee.
So tired, so cold.
Lord, I need a new coat,
not polyester, but wool,
new and pure
like the little lamb
I killed tonight.
With my right hand,
that same hand that hits
with such force,
I push myself up gently.
I know what I'd like—
some hot cocoa by the heater.

Once home, I stand at the kitchen sink,
letting the water run
till it overflows the pot,
then I remember the blood
in the bathroom
and so upstairs.
I take cleanser,

begin to scrub
the tub, tiles, the toilet bowl,
then the bathroom.
Mop, vacuum, and dust rag.
Work, work for the joy of it,
for the black boys
who know too much,
but not enough to stay away,
and sometimes a girl, the girls too.
How their hands
grab at my ankles, my knees.
and don't I lead them
like a good shepherd?
I stand at the sink,
where the water is still
overflowing the pot,
turn off the faucet,
then heat the water and sit down.
After the last sweet mouthful of chocolate
burns its way down my throat,
I open the library book,
the one on mythology,
and begin to read.
Saturn, it says, devours his children.
Yes, it's true, I know it.
An ordinary man, though, a man like me
eats and is full.
Only God is never satisfied.

The Man with the Saxophone

New York. Five A.M.
The sidewalks empty.
Only the steam
pouring from the manhole covers seems alive,
as I amble from shop window to shop window,
sometimes stopping to stare, sometimes not.
Last week's snow is brittle now
and unrecognizable as the soft, white hair
that bearded the face of the city.
I head farther down Fifth Avenue
toward the thirties,
my mind empty
like the Buddhists tell you is possible
if only you don't try.
If only I could
turn myself into a bird
like the shaman I was meant to be,
but I can't,
I'm earthbound
and solitude is my companion,
the only one you can count on.
Don't, don't try to tell me otherwise.
I've had it all and lost it
and I never want it back,
only give me this morning to keep,
the city asleep
and there on the corner of Thirty-fourth and Fifth,
the man with the saxophone,
his fingerless gloves caked with grime,
his face also,
the layers of clothes welded to his skin.
I set down my case,

he steps backward
to let me know I'm welcome,
and we stand a few minutes
in the silence so complete
I think I must be somewhere else, not here,
not in this city, this heartland of pure noise.
Then he puts the sax to his lips again
and I raise mine.
I suck the air up from my diaphragm
and bend over into the cold, golden reed,
waiting for the notes to come,
and when they do,
for that one moment,
I'm the unencumbered bird of my imagination,
rising only to fall back
toward concrete,
each note a black flower,
opening, mercifully opening
into the unforgiving new day.

The Rumored Conversation with Oneself Continues in Pittsburgh

and also a city with quiet pockets
stashed in the hubbub, like this one,

riverside at the base of the cablecars,
where we speak softly about time and space,

two rivers rushing from us as the Ohio does,
whose source is the Point we watch

from Frank's old Chevy, as warm Monongahela
and mountain-iced Allegheny merge blueblack

to vanish braided at the horizon.
What with ground glow, and flecks of city shimmer,

these water streets have more spangle
tonight than the sky. No meteors either,

though the Lyrids are past due.
The moon is nowhere; a hunch in the blackness.

Frank demonstrates its path on steering wheel
and jutting stick shift, telling the lunar opus

so deftly simple, I want to cry.
It's the way Pittsburghers play basketball,

or study Rilke: forging the rudest given
into calm, daily wages, mixing mill and bar

with the *Origin of Species,* discussing Proust
in the stands before a hockey match,

knowing the mind is a hard, slick muscle
toned by thought. And when I confess

that I've been thinking about cuffs all day,
how our joints are cuffs a-swill with fluid,

and how the shape of cuff and bone-end
rule what sort, and how much, motion

will happen, and how the muscles
are bundles of string, across and through

and about the joints, at a twitch
hitching up the marionette of our bones,

for once I feel stark raving sane,
as we sit beneath the small lean-to of wonder,

letting our minds flicker quietly together.
We are talking about drift, our own

and the continents' that clashed like stallions
to be Colorado or Tibet; how women

are marsupials; and early man thought fire
an animal he could only capture.

This is not an odd way to pass evening
in the largest inland riverport town,

but how strange to chat blithely about space
travel, in a Chevrolet whose back seat

sounds like a broken dinette set,
and mauled front seat looks driven to hysteria.

Across the river, a sandstorm of light:
buildings, arc lamps, staggering cars—

too dazzling for any one eyeful to snare.
Somewhere in the lit Oz of a city hospital,

a surgeon is breaking open the shrouded box
of a woman's chest, and reaching

a gloved hand into its snug, lonely muscle,
while she dreams of standing with Julius Caesar

across from the delta skyscrapers
and barges, the train unzipping the night

at such speed, the tunnels and waterworks,
the time-and-motion boys, the computers,

and steam rising from the street vents,
rising from the single sweat gland

under the city, above which a million people
sleep through all the tiny lay-offs

in the cell, dream in the silent architecture
of nerve and bone, people who have not yet forgotten

how to wish, who are awed by the space shuttle,
but not by their own throbbing honeycomb of light

bridging three rivers and gyrating to eye's limit.
She would stand him, mouth agape,

under the moonless sky, across from night-burning mills
spewing raw fire back at the blackness,

across from a city whose incandescence
obscures even the most frantic stars.

Lines Written in a Pittsburgh Skyscraper

It has taken me three years
to come to this view.
I know now that the body
is a river, whose bones and muscles
and organs are flowing.
I have watched their shapes
in the molded Allegheny,
contained and onrushing, below bridge
after bridge vertebra to the Ohio,
a brown river that still
powers the mind, lying long
in the trestle arms of this city
whose sentence is hard labor.

Eye level atop a church
across the street, St. Benedict the Moor
stands open armed and giant,
his back turned to the fuming
of a ghetto where some evenings
the brightest vision
is the flash of a streetlamp
on a jogger's white Nikes.

At night, the red sirens
spinning mute across the river
converge like pulsars
at some accident or crime.
An hour later, one pulls off,
hovers at a distance.
All is gesture and sign.

My students are the children
of coal miners, who watch the ground
swallow their fathers each day,
sometimes even digesting
the trapped men, turning their bones
back into lime, into coal.
It is the oldest fear:
that Earth may recall you.

Along the top of Mount Washington
lies a stole of color
unnatural to sky. Twilight's blue collar.
But the mountains are a fishing
village: steep, hearty, and solid.
At night, the lights and stars
from my window make the cityscape
an Ethiopian bride. As cars bolt
around a curve of streetlamps,
their shadows flash from under them
like sprung souls. And the river
churning its wet whispery thighs,
the river pouring blood dark
under the bridges, in the river
I find my astonished limbs
and all the stateless gels within me,
carnal, mute, wholly flowing,
unburdened toward a distant shore.

The Suicide

I. The Grey Man Tests His Idea

as his pink feet cling to the granite ledge of the State Building.
A sweep of wings sprout from his back just the way he dreamed it.
Not even his hunched assistant,
Looking out the window
Knows how it all began.
Going back in time

II. The Grey Man Invents

a way for people to fly.
Below, the ticker-tape city!
White spermatozoa of shredded paper
Teasing tiny eggy flecks
Descend into the deep.
But what if he falls

III. The Grey Man Thinks

but the sun cracks open his shiny head, and out spills
Fishing, His Girlfriend With Glasses,
The Time He Dented His Father's Car With A Tire-Iron.
The skyscrapers seem like giant whales
Rising upward from the ocean floor.
Amidst a baleen curtain

IV. The Grey Man Feels

like he's going down.
He makes a few revolutions like floating volvox

Rotating, dizzying dots,
Spinning through fluid,
His red tie flapping like a deflated parachute
While he remembers:
The building is too high for
Trilobites, Dart-like belemnites, cuttlefish,
No—
Breakfast, Lunch and Dinner,
No—
He is mixing with the wind
With volcanic gas
With hot puckering mud
With no people.

This invention doesn't work.

He is starting over.

Judith Baumel

Doing Time in Baltimore

In the south of the city on a cold rainy February day
we visited, deliberate tourists in the city where we lived,
the Babe Ruth Birthplace and Shrine Museum,
and the Poe grave. Not much, one nor the other,
though that day enlarges brighter each day
passing, to what seems my one happy day
in Baltimore, a day carved out against
the reduced joys of a lonely year in graduate school.

I kept Edgar and the Babe as small
icons proving the valuable universe might still swirl
from a daydream of my Bronx adolescence.
The cottage that housed Virginia Poe's last day
sat just off the Concourse. In front
was a gazebo strewn with dealers and the stuff
of their sullen art. A mile away past Krum's variety of nuts
and soda fountain, past Loews's twinkling ceiling
under which my high-school class graduated one June day
into the world, past the courthouse, the House That Ruth Built
declared itself pure white and green.

That day in Baltimore we walked a few blocks.
In the narrow row-house museum, I was dazed
to learn we could have bought a home run
(a fund raiser) to be ours forever as if
it were our own achievement.

Then, making it through each day,
as I did for two hundred and seventy days,
was achievement enough for me.
But in truth even a random single day, any day,
still is: the body's natural day

spirals out longer, contracts again and finally
rests, an old cuckoo spring pulled too far,
pulled one hour past what clocks call
when they call it a day.
A diurnal distortion we live in,
our bodies pushing out while the clocks pull in
in a struggle that becomes our dream of days.

Judith Baumel

Thumbs Up

On certain fall mornings it is possible to walk Eighteenth
from Tenth to First into a white sun blinding the tunneled street.
From within that obliterating light, come shades,
figures loading and unloading cargo, holding briefcases or babies,
leaning on fire trucks. The hints of two seasons cross in the air,
as, on either end of the extreme school year,
shuffling curious September or restless June,
the humid New York heat will descend on classrooms
where even under high ceilings the thick air becomes torture.
Onto the old half-varnished seats little legs pour moisture
through the clean wool plaid of new school clothes, thinking
New Year's, thinking Columbus Day, thinking Thanksgiving,
or through cotton sundresses, waiting for hydrants and hoses and pool
and the teacher despairing, shuts the lights for an illusion of coolness
In the gift of half dark children rest their heads on desks, some brood
some notice the vegetable smell of soft old wood.
They all begin Thumbs Up: Heads down, fists closed, thumbs
up, one child wanders the room to touch a random waiting thumb
whose owner may go down the hall to the water fountain,
return, and touch another, and so through slow and slower time
all thumbs, all mouths are touched, each knowing
the approach of the next, subtly, through that dark flow,
each growing up into the shuffle of new mornings gnarled
with purpose, out on the streets, watching the world's
business emerge from the shadows, come into relief, stop caught,
go past, and be finally as brilliant, seen backward, as Plato taught.

Lucie Brock-Broido

The Last Passenger Pigeon in the Cincinnati Zoo

An annulment of a species is as keen
As a monocle held up to the sun catching a page

On fire. I would woo
You if I could, bend back open like a mythic

Bird baring her neck, backed up against a hawthorn
Bough, all yours. This is not to be held against me—

This mere yearning & fondness I have
For the Beautiful—even if my labors should be

Unscored by your yellow eye, even if obedience
Should be taken as an anesthesia before imagination

Run amok, or sophistry—Angel, biscuit, nice little piece
Of traffic. Even if my efforts should be misconstrued

I will go on forgiving your
Extinction, your offense, like nobody's

Business, like your cassia carnations blooming helplessly
In April's carrion, in an onion snow when every wild

Thing is extinguished by the dog days of a season
Run amok. Once, the midwestern sky was so thick

With migrations, we blocked the sun, gun
Metal grey, shot down & shipped

To the city in barrelfulls. Our odd
Marriage is the moment of the last night

Of the last day of the last passenger
Pigeon who died out in a dull spring of 1914—

The unreeling last survivor in the Cincinnati Zoo
At the beginning of your century, when you

Were unfading, beautifully. On that anonymous
Awkward strutting night, wheeling

Out of a city's silver midst, the last
Bird died out, monogamous & willful, no

Survivors—there will be no more
Carriers with their small white billed

Messages. I was willing
To wait for you like that, in the spools

Of decades come undone like button thread unravelling, a classi
Case of an unfolding species unwinding, beautifully.

Marilyn Chin

Song of the Sad Guitar

for Maxine Hong Kingston

In the bitter year of 1988 I was banished to San Diego, California, to become a wife there. It was summer. I was buying groceries under the Yin and Yang sign of Safeway. In the parking lot, the puppies were howling to a familiar tune on a guitar plucked with the zest and angst of the sixties. I asked the player her name.

She answered:
"Stone Orchid, but if you call me that, I'll kill you."
I said:
"Yes, perhaps stone is too harsh for one with a voice so pure."
She said:
"It's the 'orchid' I detest; it's prissy, cliche and forever pink."

From my shopping bag I handed her a Tsing Tao and urged her to play on.

She sang about hitchhiking around the country, moons and lakes, homeward-honking geese, scholars who failed the examination. Men leaving for war; women climbing the watchtower. There were courts, more courts and innermost courts, and scions who pillaged the country.

Suddenly, I began to feel deeply about my own banishment. The singer I could have been, what the world looked like in spring, that Motown collection I lost. I urged her to play on:

Trickle, trickle, the falling rain.
Ming, ming, a deer lost in the forest.
Surru, surru, a secret conversation.
Hung, hung, a dog in the yard.

Then, she changed her mood, to a slower lament, trilled a
song macabre, about death, about a guitar case that opened like
a coffin. Each string vibrant, each note a thought. Tell me, Or-
chid, where are we going? "The book of changes does not signify
change. The laws are immutable. Our fates are sealed." Said
Orchid—the song is a dirge and an awakening.

Two years after our meeting, I became deranged. I couldn't
cook, couldn't clean. My house turned into a pigsty. My children
became delinquents. My husband began a long, lusty affair with
another woman. The house burned during a feverish *Santa Ana*
as I sat in a pink cranny above the garage singing, "At twenty,
I marry you. At thirty, I begin hating everything that you do."

One day while I was driving down Mulberry Lane, a voice
came over the radio. It was Stone Orchid. She said, "This is a
song for an old friend of mine. Her name is Mei Ling. She's a
warm and sensitive housewife now living in Hell's Creek, Cal-
ifornia. I've dedicated this special song for her, 'The Song of
the Sad Guitar.' "

I am now beginning to understand the song within the song,
the weeping within the willow. And you, out there, walking,
talking, seemingly alive—may truly be dead and waiting to be
summoned by the sound of the sad guitar.

Composed Near the Bay Bridge
(after a wild party)

1)
Amerigo has his finger on the pulse of China.
He, Amerigo, is dressed profoundly punk:
Mohawk-pate, spiked dog collar, black leather thighs.
She, China, freshly hennaed and boaed, is intrigued
with the new diaspora and the sexual freedom
called *bondage.* "Isn't *bondage,* therefore,
a *kind* of freedom?" she asks wanly.

2)
Thank God there was no war tonight.
Headbent, Amerigo plucks his bad guitar.
The Sleeping Giant snores with her mouth agape
while a lone nightingale trills on a tree.

Through the picture window, I watch the traffic
hone down to a quiver. Loneliness. Dawn.
A few geese winging south; minor officials return home.

Nicholas Christopher

5°

Down the long avenues the north wind
doubles over the strongest men.

Everything has turned to iron:
buildings, pavement, the stunted trees.

Even the sky, from which lapis stars glint,
painful to the naked eye.

But for the clouds of their breath,
a man and his dog might be statues.

The pretzel vendor, his fingers brittle,
rakes his coals and sucks on a chip of ice.

In an archway, under a slanting hat,
a young woman is lighting a cigarette.

There is nothing in her eyes but the spit
of flame—amber enclosing a crimson thread—

as her shadow slips away, into a waiting car,
and the sidewalk swallows her up.

The smoke of her cigarette lingers,
coiling and floating across the street

intact—a halo that hovers all night
beneath the parapet of the church

where the angel with feverish eyes
snatches it up at dawn as the snow

begins to fall, and places it—heavy
as marble suddenly—behind his head.

April in New York

1.

Vapor is curling from the manhole
like a snake from a basket.
Rain curtains the windows.
A girl made up as Mussolini—
twenty medals across her chest—
waves an Ethiopian flag and goose-steps
to martial music on a flatbed truck.
Behind the wheel, a man in whiteface
wearing a fez whispers sweet nothings
to a blow-up doll of Brigitte Bardot
in a see-through raincoat.
The charcoal sky, smeared purple,
is crisscrossed with sailboats.
It's springtime: from Inwood
to the Battery, the crowds
are restless, tossing confetti.

2.

How many false prophets will shamble
from furnished rooms today
to preach the Gospel on littered corners
or thump their Korans in caged windows?
Last night the planet Mars,
ascendant in the west, burnt
a pinhole—ruby-brilliant—
through a curtain of storm clouds.
A girl in a see-through raincoat
was murdered on East Fourth Street
by a panhandler with a mandolin.

His hair was dyed chlorophyll green
and his purple cape was embroidered
with sailboats in a moonlit expanse.
Speaking garbled Ethiopic, he confessed
to the police, but insisted
(through an interpreter)
that it was a crime of passion.

3.
It's the month of suicides.
Everybody wants something
and nobody knows where to get it.
Or why it would make any difference
in the long run if they did.
A man in a green fez and purple zoot suit
has tacked up a photo of Brigitte Bardot
in his cell in the Tombs;
he claims he's a political prisoner
writing the true history of Mussolini's
invasion of Ethiopia in 1936.
Outside his barred window the streets
of Chinatown teem with angry crowds.
A girl in whiteface is strumming
a mandolin in the driving rain
and singing love songs in Italian—
as if her life depended on it.

Nicholas Christopher

After Hours

The man who mops the floor of the luncheonette
at 2 A.M. when everyone's gone home is talking
to himself again, puffing a cigarette, listening
to Christmas carols on the radio, and pausing
before the calendar pinup that the cook has taped
below his chopping block (a wide-eyed woman wearing
only a pink cowboy hat, holster, and six-guns) while
computing the amount of cash he will have left over
from his pay check after seeing to his rent, utilities,
and such incidentals as the payment on his late
wife's hospital bills and the installment on his
car that no longer starts (what's left will be eleven
dollars to underwrite his pack-a-day of cigarettes
and a lottery ticket)—all the while continuing
to mop the floor, around the stools, between booths,
under tables, into the rest rooms, the harsh ammonia
fumes from the pail biting into the back of his throat.

Sometimes, on nights like this, when the moon
has risen over the office buildings, and the sharp
wind is rattling the cages on the storefronts,
and the freshly fallen snow has not yet been blackened
by rush-hour traffic, he locks up the luncheonette,
puts up his collar, and takes the long way around to
the subway. Past the public park with the Civil War
general stiff on horseback and the pigeons huddled
sleeping in the trees. Past warehouses where icicles,
like stalactites, drip from gutters eight storeys up.
Down by the river for a single block, where he can gaze
along the path the moonlight follows to the opposite
shore—the murk of barges, wharves, and factories,
the rusted freighters, illuminated for an instant like

the blue panes in a stained glass window that depicts
a redemption scene—before he completes his detour,
turning back into the darkness, the iron stairwell to
the subway on which his heavy boots do not make a sound.

Amy Clampitt

Amaranth and Moly

The night we bailed out Jolene from Riker's Island
tumbleweeds in such multitudes were blowing through the dark
it might almost have been Wyoming. Built like a willow
or a John Held flapper, from the shoulders up
she was pure Nefertiti, and out of that divine
brown throat came honey and cockleburs.
She wore a headcloth like a tiara above a sack dress
improvised from a beach towel. She'd turned larceny
against the bureaucracy into an art form.
When they raised the subway fare and simultaneously
cut back on Human Resources, Jolene
began jumping turnstiles as a matter of principle.
The police caught up with her at approximately
the fifteenth infraction, and the next thing
anybody knew, she'd been carted off
to the Women's House of D.
        Now that it's
been shifted to the other side of the East River,
bailing anybody out becomes an all-night expedition—
a backhanded kind of joyride, comparable
to crossing the Styx or the Little Big Horn
in a secondhand Volkswagen. You enter a region
of landfill, hamburger loess, a necropolis
of coffee grounds, of desiccated *Amaranthus albus*
(rudely known as pigweed) on the run.
No roots. When a tumbleweed takes off, barbed wire
won't stop it, much less a holstered guard
or signs reading No Authorized Vehicles
Beyond This Point. A shuttlebus arrives
after a while to cart you to the reception area,
where people paid to do it teach you how to wait,
with no message, while one shift goes off

and the next comes on, and every half hour or so
you feed another batch of change into a pay phone,
jiggling all the levers of influence you can think of
to no effect whatever. At a little after
three a.m., finally, Jolene came out—
the same beautiful outrageous gingersnap
with a whole new catalog of indictments.
On the shuttlebus, while a pimp was softly
lecturing his sullen girl on what to do next time,
Jolene described how at the precinct
they'd begun by giving her a
Psychiatric Assessment for which the City
then proceeded to bill her.
By the time the van arrived to take her
to the House of D., the officer
who'd brought her in the first place
was saying, "Jolene, I love you." And she'd
told him, she told us, exactly what he could do.
All around us in the dark of Riker's Island
the tumbleweeds scurrying were no pigweed,
I was thinking, but the amaranth of antiquity.
And Jolene was not only amaranth and moly, she was poetry
leaping the turnstiles of another century.

#2, Shoes

You could cry
for such variety
or the sad opera
of fluorescent light
falling on them,
as if it mattered
(high antennae-heeled
shoes and shoes in dalmatian
spots and shoes the color
of a day last winter, when
the tired snow crusted
over stacked copies
of the *Daily News,*
and white-striped gutters
all over town).

You might watch
for the sand colored
prints each pair leaves
behind, in unison,
the one and only thing
they agree upon.

You could pray
for a single pair
of ruby slippers
in the hoard,
to sing their red song out of key,
enormous, wailing against
the din of train
and shuffle, of wrappers and silk,

of soggy shopping bags
and distant rain.

When the train comes
and all the pairs unite
in a single sigh
of leather or cloth,
all of them
aboard, skipstop service,
toward 34th, 42nd, and faster,
all the way to 72nd and a roster
of other points north,
you know
they are going to eat at Ollie's,
on 116th Street,
they are going to Columbia University,
they are going to buy crack,
they are going to visit a newborn baby,
they are going to buy more shoes,
or take a tap class.

Look up
and see the moon-faced owners,
trying not to look at you. Looking,
in fact, downward
at the newly inside bright-lit
way their shoes have begun to shine
in the train light,
as though filled with hope,
as though thinking, softly,
now, finally,
they are getting somewhere.

Elizabeth Cohen

Drive-By Shooting

By the time you read this
the umber stains
will be washed away, the rivulets
and estuaries born
from the bullet's impact
will be replaced by a clean lake
of new glass. A new picture
will be up on the calendar
(a Vermont winter scene,
children with sleds)
and somewhere a million lightyears
from Los Angeles, a supernova
will be born.

in the fire lane

we are deadly decadent anarchists
living in the fire lane
you know that
we do not secure the lives
we mean to lead

because we are narcissists
I use us
because loss is personal
we don't even watch or listen
for the news
we are moving fast
we like the pleasures
the facts suggest knowing
abandonment

we are deadly in our way
the way we forget, fall asleep
fall out, leave the door open
the men with unhealed wounds
jump us, try to maim us
without even taking the bread
without even, as Wesley says,
anything "motivational"

this happened to me
and someone known to me
on the same night
have we been listening
did we hear the scream in the hall
or Ntozake say, "every three minutes"
did i know the woman

who met the mugger
on the same night
was shot for saying no
like i did

he took my head
in his hands
and bashed it to the wall
"yes, that's right, bitch"
smacked off my glasses
his brass ring cut its way
through my mouth to the gum
moved my teeth
"i'm gonna kill you"

i thought i was a doll
with a porcelain face
shattering off

i screamed
i die my way
a kick to the groin
i screamed six flights

too late but they came
he ran 'cause they came yelling
in T-shirts and drawers
canes and switchblades
the woman across the hall
barefoot with kitchen knife
and a new lover behind her

but some of us just wait
for the song to be gone
feeling taken by force
we are decadent, yes
because we know
have sat through terror
outside a window

we cannot do this fast enough
no time to write the poem
just time to say
we have got to be safe
we cannot afford the oblivion
we talk so much about

if i'm not there
you could be gone
if you don't save me
i could be lost
we have to do
here living in the fire lane
where it all moves fast
the emergency is ongoing

the song will have to
have the passion
we dispense instead of dreams
the song will have to mean
having somewhere to go
and the freedom
to move up the street
that goes there

Connie Deanovich

I am a woman in a red blouse
blushing to have to admit my
glowing autumn moon

has left the large backyard I
live in in my mind
There's a truck there now
yellow and black like a can

of tobacco
Idling
its engines are ready to burn

to blaze across the country
like resurrection sunshine

My books are in this truck:
Alice in Wonderland
Go Ask Alice
The Autobiography of Alice B. Toklas
Alice Ordered Me to Be Made

Big Top
By the Shores of Gitchigoomi
and the rest

I'm shipping them to a tiny library
in Truth or Consequences, New Mexico
so that I can begin the life that
starts with apple picking and
ends with zigzagging down the street

Then I'll be a woman in a red blouse
blushing to have to admit my adventures
have landed me in a novel that makes
my friend a million dollars in
R-rated movie rights

The glowing autumn movie screen
at the Drive-In will entertain the
truckers who idle away two hours

chewing tobacco and watching my life
on the giant fireproof screen
blazing momentarily like

a temperamental crystal in the
temperamental sunshine

Connie Deanovich

Road Block: Santa Fe, New Mexico

I had good manners
and waited until we passed
before taking pictures from Kathy's car

The policemen
in Nazi-black uniforms, gloves,
and boots, double-barreled shotguns
poised behind semis

so hot
not a tree in sight
no water, little sound
adobe-penitentiary glazing in heat
just before the mesa went red

This is too western
way too meaty, like a pig
baked underground

I'm reselling my square of the blanket
Jimenez was found in
and the patch of Governor's grass
where his partner died crouching

This is too western
I'm selling my pictures:
a pushed-back policeman's hat radioing in,
the red flashlight waving us on

National Assessment

by the light of a female impersonator
the message is clear and
smooth as fish stone
action is called for
we must check and recheck
as if an elephant just turned the corner

as a nation
are our seams straight?
who are we by Blue Moon?
how are our people honeymooning
if no longer by visiting the highway?
what will become of the drive-in?

we were we are
apple pie apple
at least a drag queen sports tits you know not to count on
at least once everyday in bed someone whispers *fabulous* to
someone else but we can't hear this exchange
and there's a lot of other treasure that is lost to us

as a nation
do we all carry a lost city in our hearts?
whether underwater or blown into particles is immaterial
so long as each and every one of us longs for a visit
so long as we all have visions of gold and unisex tunics
without a lost city to lose our hearts to we ourselves are lost

our nation's drag queens make our nation the nation it is
or wants to be or tries to become or pretends its way into being
and for a national stamp perhaps the next should be Divine

goddess of so many youths and not so youths
we need a national symbol that tells the citizenry to distrust
while at the same time to smile and to try and copy the moves

In Praise of New York

As we rise above it, row after row
Of lights reveal the incredible size
Of our loss. An ideal commonwealth
Would be no otherwise,
For we can no more legislate
Against the causes of unhappiness,
Such as death or impotence or times
When no one notices,
Than we can abolish the second law
Of thermodynamics, which states
That all energy, without exception, is wasted.
Still, under certain conditions
It is possible to move
To a slightly nicer
Neighborhood. Or if not,
Then at least there is usually someone
To talk to, or a library
That stays open till nine.
And any night you can see Times Square
Tremulous with its busloads
Of tourists who are seeing all of this
For the first and last time
Before they are flown
Back to the republic of Azerbaidzhan
On the shore of the Caspian,
Where for weeks they will dream of our faces
Drenched with an unbelievable light.

Tom Disch

The Argument Resumed;
or, Up through Tribeca

It may not be forever, but
The zing of beauty in the middle
Of the day—this little kid, for instance,
Heading home in his stroller,
Radiantly silly in a knitted snowsuit,
Or those windows of snazzy bowls
A few blocks back, all of solid wood
But gleaming as from a kiln
(Somebody should pay good money for that.
Ah, to be rich!) . . . The zing, I say,
An dich as we take our constitutional
Does add a luster when a luster is needed,
And if that luster fades as we proceed
Elsewhere, there's no call to be
Bereft. We are left with our store
Of memories: the scent, maybe, of a herbal rinse
Familiar from childhood. Or the sky may echo
The blue of a favorite tie. But "forever"?
Doesn't that tend to detract from the glory
Of the thing? Glory must burst
On us like fireworks. If the gleam
Or the sweetness isn't fleeting,
How shall it bear repeating?
How should we dare to eat another
Sundae of sunsets? See where a peach
Glows among other peaches in the fruitbowl.
Such and no other is the soul.

Harbor Lights

I'm coming home through the red lacquered lobby,
    corridors the bitter green of gingko
        marred by the transoms' milky light.

I am sixteen and the room's three-fifty a night
    in the Chinese hotel on Water Street,
        and I've been out again to the grocery

where they sell cigarettes, one for a dime,
    and to look at the stone face
        in the shop window. I'm calling her

the angel, the mother of angels, and chiseled
    upon the marble of her face is a veil
        so thin it isn't stone at all

but something that emerges out of her chill dreaming.
    It's like watching your mother sleep,
        minutes after you have been conceived,

and her closed eyes say it's all right
    to wake alone, almost at evening, in a city hotel
        where all night from the room next door

comes the sound, I swear, of chopping.
    It's the room of the old woman
        the men at the desk call Mama, and the best

I can imagine is that she's working late
    for the café down the block,
        cleaving celery, splitting the white

and acid green of bok choi. All day
     she'll wash the floors in the halls,
          hissing to herself in sounds I imagine

are curses, damning the residue of the streets
     the residents track all night
          onto the speckled constellations

of the linoleum. She scrubs until it's flawless
     as black water off the piers down the block,
          until the floors gleam green under the window

where RESIDENTIAL shimmers, watery electric
     shantung blossoming over and over
          two stories above the street.

Nights like this, when it's raining
     and the chill seems almost visible,
          coming in across the Sound and the waterfront's

rambling warehouses, the radiator pronounces,
     almost exactly, my mother's name.
          Then the pipes with their silver garlands

sing *runaway*. I've taken the pill I bought
     on the corner, where someone's always reciting
          the litany of an impossible future:

Purple Doubledome, Blue Microdot, Sunshine.
     I'm waiting for the flowers in the cracked linoleum
          to twist and open, scrubbed into blossom,

waiting for the harbor lights
     to burn—the night caught in my hotel window
          like a piece of film in a projector,

melting, so that light comes searing out of the darkness
     first as boiling pinpricks, then a whole angel.
          What I've bought is nothing, aspirin

or sugar, but I don't know that,
    and I'm waiting to come on. It's raining harder,
      the knife in the next room striking

the block, the glass beading up
    and then erasing itself, shimmering the lights,
      and the stone face around the corner

dreams her way out of the world
    of appearances behind her window,
      her glaze of rain, her veil.

Mark Doty

Broadway

Under Grand Central's tattered vault
    —maybe half a dozen electric stars still lit—
      one saxophone blew, and a sheer black scrim

billowed over some minor constellation
    under repair. Then, on Broadway, red wings
      in a storefront tableau, lustrous, the live macaws

preening, beaks opening and closing
    like those animated knives that unfold all night
      in jewelers' windows. For sale,

glass eyes turned out toward the rain,
    the birds lined up like the endless flowers
      and cheap gems, the makeshift tables

of secondhand magazines
    and shoes the hawkers eye
      while they shelter in the doorways of banks.

So many pockets and paper cups
    and hands reeled over the weight
      of that glittered pavement, and at 103rd

a woman reached to me across the wet roof
    of a stranger's car and said, *I'm Carlotta,*
      I'm hungry. She was only asking for change,

so I don't know why I took her hand.
    The rooftops were glowing above us,
      enormous, crystalline, a second city

lit from within. That night
      a man on the downtown local stood up
            and said, *My name is Ezekiel,*

I am a poet, and my poem this evening is called
      fall. He stood up straight
            to recite, a child reminded of his posture

by the gravity of his text, his hands
      hidden in the pockets of his coat.
            Love is protected, he said,

the way leaves are packed in snow,
      the rubies of fall. God is protecting
            the jewel of love for us.

He didn't ask for anything, but I gave him
      all the change left in my pocket,
            and the man beside me, impulsive, moved,

gave Ezekiel his watch.
      It wasn't an expensive watch,
            I don't even know if it worked,

but the poet started, then walked away
      as if so much good fortune
            must be hurried away from,

before anyone realizes it's a mistake.
      Carlotta, her stocking cap glazed
            like feathers in the rain,

under the radiant towers, the floodlit ramparts,
      must have wondered at my impulse to touch her,
            which was like touching myself,

the way your own hand feels when you hold it
      because you want to feel contained.
            She said, *You get home safe now, you hear?*

In the same way Ezekiel turned back
    to the benevolent stranger.
       I will write a poem for you tomorrow,

he said. *The poem I will write will go like this:*
    Our ancestors are replenishing
       the jewel of love for us.

A Hill of Beans

One spring the circus gave
free passes and there was music,
the screens unlatched
to let in starlight. At the well,
a monkey tipped her his fine red hat
and drank from a china cup.
By mid-morning her cobblers
were cooling on the sill.
Then the tents folded and the grass

grew back with a path
torn waist-high to the railroad
where the hoboes jumped the slow curve
just outside Union Station.
She fed them while they talked,
easy in their rags. *Any two points
make a line,* they'd say,
and we're gonna ride them all.

Cat hairs
came up with the dipper;
Thomas tossed on his pillow
as if at sea. When money failed
for peaches, she pulled
rhubarb at the edge of the field.
Then another man showed up
in her kitchen and she smelled
fear in his grimy overalls,
the pale eyes bright as salt.

There wasn't even pork
for the navy beans. But he ate

straight down to the blue
bottom of the pot and rested
there a moment, hardly breathing.
That night she made Thomas
board up the well.
Beyond the tracks, the city blazed
as if looks were everything.

The Satisfaction Coal Company

1.

What to do with a day.
Leaf through *Jet*. Watch T.V.
Freezing on the porch
but he goes anyhow, snow too high
for a walk, the ice treacherous.
Inside, the gas heater takes care of itself;
he doesn't even notice being warm.

Everyone says he looks great
Across the street a drunk stands smiling
at something carved in a tree.
The new neighbor with the floating hips
scoots out to get the mail
and waves once, brightly,
storm door clipping her heel on the way in.

2.

Twice a week he had taken the bus down Glendale hill
to the corner of Market. Slipped through
the alley by the canal and let himself in.
Started to sweep
with terrible care, like a woman
brushing shine into her hair,
same motion, same lullaby.
No curtains—the cop on the beat
stopped outside once in the hour
to swing his billy club and glare.

It was better on Saturdays
when the children came along;

he mopped while they emptied
ashtrays, clang of glass on metal
then a dry scutter. Next they counted
nailheads studding the leather cushions.
Thirty-four! they shouted,
that was the year and
they found it mighty amusing.

But during the week he noticed more—
lights when they gushed or dimmed
at the Portage Hotel, the 10:32
picking up speed past the B & O switchyard,
floorboards trembling and the explosive
kachook kachook kachook kachook
and the oiled rails ticking underneath.

3.
They were poor then but everyone had been poor.
He hadn't minded the sweeping,
just the thought of it—like now
when people ask him what he's thinking
and he says *I'm listening.*

Those nights walking home alone,
the bucket of coal scraps banging his knee,
he'd hear a roaring furnace
with its dry, familiar heat. Now the nights
take care of themselves—as for the days,
there is the canary's sweet curdled song,
the wino smiling through his dribble.
Past the hill, past the gorge
choked with wild sumac in summer,
the corner has been upgraded.
Still, he'd like to go down there someday
to stand for a while, and get warm.

Cornelius Eady

Romare Bearden Retrospective at The Brooklyn Museum

Opera! All that cardboard
And newsprint roars, a chorus:
Sweat, Jazz and Jesus,
Big women lifting their skirts,

A hot breeze down 125th Street,
Subways demonstrating the snake dance,
Cigars, bop and the numbers,
The infra-red tenements
(Cigarette lighters of the Gods),

Murder, pig meat, and let's not forget
The vertigo which powers the trumpets,
The lightning the drummers twirl above their heads,
The concealed weapons and still-born patents.

Here's the nervous tic of a culture we thought
We checked at the door,
The headlines of a world
That threatens to rip open.

Barbara Elovic

Brooklyn Bound

As if posed for a picture called "Restless Youth"

three kids stand on the footbridge
that spans the Stillwell Avenue station
and look out past the trains and the concession

stands of Coney Island—Nathan's Famous, a shrine built
to the hot dog, and Disco Beat Bumper Cars—
toward the ocean and the subtler blue of the sky.

Did they catch the Mermaid Parade
that afternoon on the Boardwalk?
Women and girls in glitter and green blankets

enthroned in wagons and wheelchairs,
flapped their fin-bound legs
when reminded by their mothers

welcoming summer to Brooklyn shores.
As the mermaids rolled by, the Aqua String Band played along
pulling everyone's attention off the water, the horizon

and its promise of no limits.
It's Saturday, only four o'clock—what else have they to do?
Hours of daylight before them, the kids

hesitate before boarding the train
that bends achingly, as beautiful in the arc of its tracks
as the flight of any bird, away from the water.

Discovering the Photograph of Lloyd, Earl, and Priscilla

These are the great discoveries of my middle age:
This roadhouse in Omaha where Uncle Lloyd is nursing
Highballs with an ex-G.I. named Earl.
She's here, too, leaving a damp pink parenthesis
On the rim of her glass. The men are bored
But the girl whose name hisses like an iron across damp shirts
Peels open a pack of cigarettes and fills the room with smoke.
I have always wanted a coziness like theirs:
Rain touching the roof and someone trying to explain about
    Labor—
I might have been the waitress mopping up tips with a damp
    hand,
The one who loved Earl all those years while toting armloads
Of cobblers made from berries tiny as black caviar.
Tonight in an open window someone's stylus unzips a faint
    piano.
It must be 1947, Earl slicing salted melon from the rind,
Drinking the juice off his plate and the waitress going home
To count the dresser knobs until she falls asleep.
Tonight I find I envy the rain turning Omaha to
    daguerreotype,
Mud roads running amber as the veins in bad marble.
It is getting late. In the background beyond Earl and the
    waitress
There must be gardens. Roses, bowed down by their own
    heaviness,
Each day grow more perfect and more neighborly.
There must be graves and each separate grave is sending out
Its separate ghost.

Lynn Emanuel

Desire

This is not Turner's Venice,
Not all the light is let loose across the canals,
The low clefts of little waves.
This is Pittsburgh where the air is sulphurous
And the water landlocked, slowed by waste and those small
    iron bridges.
But even here we have discovered desire, like Columbus
Who was looking for the end of the world and stumbled on
    continents.

In the elms there are supple constellations of light.
We are sitting in the yard and I, too, am hoping for the end
Of something, of the world, maybe,
That great still perfect lip and those little boats going off.

But it is August and this
The most familiar place in the world,
Calm water, boats, channels
And beautiful, too, those little bridges
Leading back and forth across the river.
Here in our own back yard we can find
The rare acres of stars, the thin wind
Abating in the huge green hesitations of the trees.

The Sleeping

I have imagined all this:
In 1940 my parents were in love
And living in the loft on West 10th
Above Mark Rothko who painted cabbage roses
On their bedroom walls the night they got married.

I can guess why he did it.
My mother's hair was the color of yellow apples
And she wore a velvet hat with her pajamas.

I was not born yet. I was remote as starlight.
It is hard for me to imagine that
My parents made love in a roomful of roses
And I wasn't there.

But now I am. My mother is blushing.
This is the wonderful thing about art.
It can bring back the dead. It can wake the sleeping
As it might have late that night
When my father and mother made love above Rothko
Who lay in the dark thinking *Roses, Roses, Roses.*

Elaine Equi

Words Read by Lightning

It was nearly eleven
when we arrived in NY
and the combination
of the storm
and the scotch
had made everyone giddy

except us.

There was one opera
in the air
and a different one
on the air

and that impressed me

as well as
the delicate manner
in which people
disposed of their garbage
carrying it
from curb to curb
as if to make it
more comfortable.

This then was a place
where many vicarious
pleasures gathered

the wood
from which I'd make
my legs

where one could lead
a thousand lives
without lifting
a finger

the hands
already full
with what is.

Elaine Equi

Breakfast with Jerome

Light shivering on its tightrope

Bizet in the background

Banana bread and a pear

Swinging its lantern of white noise

The chef's hat perches on the fence

The coachman is driving the city to the city

Magically the page refills itself

Ode to Chicago

In my city
dinosaurs are not extinct.
Evenings they stroll downtown
and their smooth bodies
from the fortieth floor
are often mistaken for golf courses.
Pterodactyls swoop
above our vegetarian restaurants
while in the park
the famous sea serpent
entices tourists with his lewd chatter,
his long neck.
Nowhere else will you find rocks that perspire,
trees that grow hair.
Here even the common criminal
loves to talk about his "primeval mother"
and although some refer to it as uncivilized,
in my city we know where we come from.
We remember our origins.

Martín Espada

Tony Went to the Bodega but He Didn't Buy Anything

para Angel Guadalupe

Tony's father left the family
and the Long Island city projects,
leaving a mongrel-skinny puertorriqueño boy
nine years old
who had to find work.

Makengo the Cuban
let him work at the bodega.
In grocery aisles
he learned the steps of the dry-mop mambo,
banging the cash register
like piano percussion
in the spotlight of Machito's orchestra,
polite with the abuelas who bought on credit,
practicing the grin on customers
he'd seen Makengo grin
with his bad yellow teeth.

Tony left the projects too,
with a scholarship for law school.
But he cursed the cold primavera
in Boston;
the cooking of his neighbors
left no smell in the hallway.
and no one spoke Spanish
(not even the radio).

So Tony walked without a map
through the city,

a landscape of hostile condominiums
and the darkness of white faces,
sidewalk-searcher lost
till he discovered the projects.

Tony went to the bodega
but he didn't buy anything:
he sat by the doorway satisfied
to watch la gente (people
island-brown as him)
crowd in and out,
hablando español,
thought: this is beautiful,
and grinned
his bodega grin.

This is a rice and beans
success story:
today Tony lives on Tremont Street,
above the bodega.

Martín Espada

Latin Night at the Pawnshop

Chelsea, Massachusetts
Christmas, 1987

The apparition of a salsa band
gleaming in the Liberty Loan
pawnshop window:

Golden trumpet,
silver trombone,
congas, maracas, tambourine,
all with price tags dangling
like the city morgue ticket
on a dead man's toe.

My Diamond Stud

He'll be a former cat burglar
because I have baubles
to lose. I'll know him
by the black
carnation he's tossing:
heads, he takes me,
stems, the same. Yes,
he'll be a hitchhiker at this
roller-rink I frequent, my diamond
stud who'll wheel up shedding
sparks & say *"Ecoutez*
bé-bé. I'm a member
of a famous folded trapeze
act. My agility is legend, etc."
keeping his jeweler's eye on
my gold fillings. He'll know
what I really want: whipping
me with flowers, his fingers' grosgrain
sanded smooth, raw
to my every move. For our tryst
we'll go to travel-folder heaven
& buff-puff each other's
calluses in valentine tubs.
He'll swindle the black heart
between my thighs
dress me up in Ultra-
suede sheaths, himself
in Naugahyde. No,
leather. He'd never
let anything touch him
that wasn't once alive.

Alice Fulton

Risk Management

Relentless escalators bore us
to this convention where we wander, homogeneous,
sinking into easy chairs
as if our hearts were made of butter. A contained fire

triggered the sprinkler system yesterday.
The burnt sienna plush turned carotene
and I foresaw venture
capitalists huddling in the crawl-
space beneath the smoke, discussing risk
management and right-of-way. Others have slipped

mirrors under doors, dreaming of listening
devices, hush
money, of money
men who speak in megamergers. Dressed in checks

and balances, we the plebiscite
long to rise above the drudge
work, pulp
work, grunt
work and rock out: to ballet, croquet
our days away in light that burns
us to the hidden quick, to be glad
in neon excess
that hits the pavement rippling
as if run through
with a fine-toothed comb.

Still, we've folded classic jackets over
our bodice-ripping
novels: conventions mean accepting as one

thing something that's another
and a different thing. I know

I'd like to astound
the man beside me with a proposition: "What say
we take the next flight to the old world,
visit Lesser-Kvetching-in-Hogsheaven?"
Instead I'm urging the never-impetuous dawn to hurry
with a morning and a plane
that will return me to the place I left. Ten years ago

I stayed up all night chopping vegetables
with denimed men and women to a rock band's beat.
Now in the great arena opposite the lobby
someone watches as 7000 gallons of water churn
with 200 of white paint to lay half
an inch of ice for tomorrow's hockey game.
I'm talking the twin enchantments:

rhythm and precision. At this minute, light from a blast
furnace tigers the foundry
worker's back. His 60-pound ladle swings sure
as an anticipated need. He moves with a ballerina's ease
and strain, allowing us to take comfort in him somewhere
between risk and safety. He's like the convention

of majorettes to lead the Labor
Day parade, zipped in vinyl thigh
boots, suits molten as new pennies
above predictable kicks, batons
that soar, catch the light and twirl
before they're caught.

Alice Fulton

The Wreckage Entrepreneur

It takes faith—this tripping through the mixed blessings
of debris with eyes peeled for the toxic
toothpaste green of copper keystones.
On good days Carborundum-bladed saws free sublime
objective blossoms; stained glass
hangs rescued and suspended
like frozen scarves on lines
behind indigents at barrel fires;
granite cherubs wearing crowbar marks
lie abandoned at her door.
After the wrecking ball
she loads her truck with crushed iotas
because cast marble dust's more durable than solid cuts.
Only occasionally, gargoyles blur
under the pressure of her gaze
as if vision were itself corrosive.
Then deco mirrors hold her
as they catacomb the warehouse walls,
and clinging at the empty
gilding of a door, she wants
a shower and lather of pumice
to melt the gritty casing of her
nakedness. How small she looks
beside what she has saved.

Travelogue

Sweetheart, I wish you could tour my native land.
Once you'd seen the dolls in peasant costume,
the unstable terrain, a landslide hanging
by a thread, you'd weather my moods and love me
in context. Even postcards are in limited
edition. You could comb curio shops for years
and never unearth an authentic print
from the ten-cent bin.

I'll unfold my map and go further.
We inhabit only the uppermost floor
of lavishly lit dwellings. Each
apartment is transparent, boasts
picture windows on all sides, no
curtains, so our postures as we
sulk in alcoves, dress or serve
dessert are decorative, illustrations
for curious passerby.

Often we appear as a congregation of silhouettes,
similar to figures painted on the walls of Egyptian tombs.
We cover pages of our datebooks with hieroglyphics,
a historic scrawl that passeth understanding.

Here in the map's upper right hand corner:
an aerial view of the maze which is our
capitol. A shuttle bus can take you even
deeper into the interior, except during
"storm and avalanche danger," the season
I'm most homesick for—to watch the sea
advance to treeline again, as it does once

annually, and flood the dear, tranquilized landscape, forming lakes in almost every depression.

Debora Greger

Piranesi in L.A.

una veduta ideata

And packing sketches, ink, knife, and quills,
down from his imagined vantage point

wound a man as in one of the rococo carriages
he'd drawn, smoothing frock coat and wig.

Foreshortened, the locked curve of freeway exit
straightens, debouching just short of a headwall

of sea—the way his prints take the specks
straggling in foreground toward vistas

of vanishing—sea into itself; canyon overrun
by morning glory gone wild; orchards turned under,

paved over; your hand pointing
to a cliff-hanging house, crossing it out.

Think of kisses the length of stoplights,
red of the WRONG WAY signs that loom before the lost

who want just to turn back
a page to the well-kept neighborhood

of the known, crisp sunlight not islanding a lawn
into an idea. On a copper plate he'd build,

backwards, *una veduta ideata,* rearranging ruins
into a history pretty or grand enough

to be lived in—or slid into an acid bath.
Beneath an entrance ramp to nothing

but unetched lanes of sky, a skater cuts
between cars through shadow's pilings.

To dodge, to touch—feather breaking air bubbles
so acid can bite, or ribbon of shade tying hands

apart—without irony, on love's lasting,
optimistic as this city where what's built wrong

goes down to earthquake, mudslide, wrecking ball
before age has its chance. Full sleeves tied back,

as he etched with the needle what he remembered,
reversed, he spoke to the plate

the anthology of decay.

Debora Greger

Air-Conditioned Air

Of windows closing on muslin curtains
so they no longer swelled into hoop skirts
or swooned across love seats

the night a taxi raced from lab to lodgings,
men in white coats thrusting a bundled blanket
at a dreamer—their swaddled ice

the first from his machine. Farewell,
ceiling fans that propelled interim regimes
into torrid zones, palm courts

fawning over wilted colonials,
aspics weeping onto the native greens.
Farewell, the flies that tended leftover meat.

Like servants shooed from table,
they wove shadow to shadow
through the vestigial dusk.

It is late. The street light
lies fair upon the strait, on the coast
of Florida it gleams. Sea turtles lay their eggs

in the parking lots of hotels
glimmering and vast—come to the window,
air-conditioned is the night air,

you can hear the comfort of its roar
begin to chill and then begin again,
the flow of something human drowning the sea

71

somewhere far below our room.
The air is calm tonight, the same air as tomorrow,
and we are here. Look how the little candelabra

of a pleasure boat is borne by the darkness
of water through the earthly dark
over the old slave route.

The Shopping-Bag Lady

You told people I would know easily what the murdered
lady had in her sack which could prove she was happy
more or less. As if they were a game, the old women
who carry all they own in bags, maybe proudly,
without homes we think except the streets.
But if I could guess (nothing in sets for example),
I would not. They are like those men who lay their
few things on the ground in a park at the end of Hester.
For sale perhaps, but who can tell? Like her way
of getting money. Never asking. Sideways and disconcerting.
With no thanks, only judgment. "You are a nice girl,"
one said as she moved away and then stopped in front
of a bum sitting on the bench who yelled that he would
kill her if she did not get away from him. She walked
at an angle not exactly away but until she was the same
distance from each of us. Stood still, looking down.
Standing in our attention as if it were a palpable thing.
Like the city itself or the cold winter. Holding her hands.
And if there was disgrace, it was God's. The failure
was ours as she remained quiet near the concrete wall
with cars coming and the sound of the subway filling
and fading in the most important place we have yet devised.

Linda Gregg

Lies and Longing

Half the women are asleep on the floor
on pieces of cardboard.
One is face down under a blanket
with her feet and ankle bracelet showing.
Her spear leans against the wall by her head
where she can reach it.
The woman who sits on a chair won't speak
because this is not her dress.
An old woman sings an Italian song in English
and says she wants her name in lights:
Faye Runaway. Tells about her grown children.
One asks for any kind of medicine.
One says she has a rock that means honor
and a piece of fur.
One woman's feet are wrapped in rags.
One keeps talking about how fat she is
so nobody will know she's pregnant.
They lie about getting letters.
One lies about a beautiful dead man.
One lies about Denver. Outside
it's Thirtieth Street and hot and no sun.

Solea

there are rapists
out there

some of them
don't like asian women
they stab them
and run off to lake tahoe
in search of more pussy
in casino parking lots

thelonious monk
reminds me of you
and i forget
about this place
it's nice

but then
i have to put in
an appearance
at family dinners
and listen to other voices
my blood
in the warm gravy
and the kiss i reserve
only for little children

i can't play
those records
all the time
thelonious monk
is only joyful
in a hurting kind
of way

there are sad men
out there
some of them
don't like me
they like to talk
about corpses and dirt
and how life used to be
so good
when they were young
in the war

i like to kiss you
like i do
little children
it tastes good
but i have to leave
the room sometimes
is deep
wanting to be crazy
and painting my toenails
gold
and seeing universes
in my colors

there are killers
out there
some of them
smile at me
they dream
about snipers on the freeway
aiming machine guns
and conga drums
at innocent drivers
in their volvos
and mustangs
and dodge darts

new york
reminds me of you
so do the locks
on my door
and the way i look
sometimes
when i feel
schizophrenic

there is real beauty
in my eyes
when i lose my mind

i understand you better
this way
and it doesn't hurt
so much

anymore

Natural Death

la lupe on the dick cavett show
refuses to discuss fidel and the cuba
she once knew
o the grandeur of it
all gone now

she's come to america
to live in her dream
gold lamé jumpsuits
and rhinestone cloaks
you can't judge a man
by the length of his

o the grandeur of it

young girls paint moustaches
on their faces
young men wear yellow satin dresses
eating star-spangled sandwiches
in the saturday night parade

and bodies are buried
in saran wrap on the beach
fragile blossoms wither on beds
in southern california heat

the toilet paper heiress is kidnapped
by mysterious forces
her mother prays in a cathedral
in the darkness of her riviera sunglasses
calling out to god
when her daughter is revealed
as robin hood

o the grandeur of it
mysterious forces
and telephone calls
from anxious mothers
in the milky way
warning all daughters to beware

beware of nightclubs
and cuban mamas
beware of the street
beware of doorbells and abortions
beware of pregnancy
beware of public transportation
beware of frozen meat
and strange men
and rabid animals
beware of strange colors
strange smells
strange sounds
strange feelings
beware of loneliness
and the rhythm
of your heartbeat

Jessica Hagedorn

Latin Music in New York

made me dance with you
tito   eddie   n ray
somewhere with plumjam eyelids
i danced with you
in a roomful of mirrors
in miss harlow's house

the white girl's in town
and i smell death
the poet dying in a bar
body shaking in time
to lady day's song
        he's dying in a nod
        in a lullaby
        of ambulance haze
        and chloral hydrate
        they burned his brain

somewhere
i saw the white girl smiling
la cucaracha was up all night
hiding her spoons   her mirrors   her revolutions
in the morning
        the trace of vampires
        still there
        in the blood   even after a bath

you can't wash it away
you can't hide it
again and again
i looked under my bed

                inside a perfume box
                        in the argentinian dagger
                                the baby wolf gave me
                                    in your eyes
                                        in a furtive smile
                                        in a good fuck
                                            in the boogaloo i do
there's no escaping it
    somewhere   with plumjam eyelids

i danced the tasty freeze shuffle with you
the reds   the blues   the tango con tu madre
it's there
in town for the night
a guest appearance   a quick solo
death gets hyped
and i'm in love again

latin music in new york
made me dance with you
azúcar y chocolaté
the alligator dream
of a tropical night

death makes a quick run
to las vegas
trying to take the poet
with him

latin music in new york
made me dance with you
tito   eddie   n ray

revolutions are creeping out
from under my bed!

and i sing a song for you
         and you
                and
                      you

Edward Hirsch

Man on a Fire Escape

He couldn't remember what propelled him
out of the bedroom window onto the fire escape
of his fifth-floor walkup on the river,

so that he could see, as if for the first time,
sunset settling down on the dazed cityscape
and tugboats pulling barges up the river.

There were barred windows glaring at him
from the other side of the street
while the sun deepened into a smoky flare

that scalded the clouds gold-vermillion.
It was just an ordinary autumn twilight—
the kind he had witnessed often before—

but then the day brightened almost unnaturally
into a rusting, burnished, purplish-red haze
and everything burst into flame;

the factories pouring smoke into the sky,
the trees and shrubs, the shadows,
of pedestrians scorched and rushing home. . . .

There were storefronts going blind and cars
burning on the parkway and steel girders
collapsing into the polluted waves.

Even the latticed fretwork of stairs
where he was standing, even the first stars
climbing out of their sunlit graves

were branded and lifted up, consumed by fire.
It was like watching the start of Armageddon,
like seeing his mother dipped in flame. . . .

And then he closed his eyes and it was over.
Just like that. When he opened them again
the world had reassembled beyond harm.

So where had he crossed to? Nowhere.
And what had he seen? Nothing. No foghorns
called out to each other, as if in a dream,

and no moon rose over the dark river
like a warning—icy, long forgotten—
while he turned back to an empty room.

Edward Hirsch

When Skyscrapers Were Invented in Chicago

I think of it as a large moment with shadows
Expanding like a summer afternoon at the lake, sunspots

Blinking on the waves and a sudden burst of sails
Shivering in the distance like a mirage, the white clouds

Billowing with heat and floating over the water for miles,
The sky an emptiness to be scribbled across and filled.

It couldn't have happened without a democratic vision
Of time, the present finally equal to the past,

"Progress before precedent," as Louis Sullivan put it,
The self-evident proclamation of a city to be built

Into the sky, the need for fireproof buildings
And rentable space, a giant who could stand for years

With his feet in the mud and his head in the clouds
Withstanding the heat of mid-July and the icy winds

That blast off the lake in late December. To be sure,
It took a couple of hundred businessmen with American

Dreams of profit and plenty of credit, visionary
Architects and engineers who wanted to get rich

And were thrilled by the ugliness and dirt, the devastation
Of a fire that had started in a barn on DeKoven Street

After the World's Fair and the Classical Revival
That destroyed Sullivan's career, New World architects

Crossing the ocean on steamers, pledging allegiance to Europe,
Even as houses, American houses, were growing on the prairie.

For the New World

(Auditorium Building, Chicago, Adler and Sullivan, 1887–1889)

The first idea was man walking through space in a tower
Of solid masonry carried on a floating foundation,
A raft weighing thirty million pounds and loaded down
With pig-iron and bricks, masses of timber and steel
Rails, three layers of I-beams. Think of it
As a farm boy planting his feet in the loose mud
And hoisting a city kid on his shoulders, a tower

Soaring on a strong Midwestern back, Adler and Sullivan's
Symphony in brick for the New World. Think of standing
At dawn on the recessed balcony above the Second City
For the first time, swaying in the wind and staring out
At the horizon-line where the lake meets the sky
On the edge of the prairie, something large and possible
In the long expanse of water and land, something blue

And plaintive in the brightening rhythms of morning,
A city to be built, the sun sweeping upwards. . . .
There is something American in the moment, something
Dark and innocent about our faith in a future rising
On the prairie, immense and open-hearted, the skeleton
Construction of skyscrapers just around the corner—
The old Schiller Building and the new Stock Exchange—

The idea of a "Garden City" growing out of rubble, the fire
That made the skyline possible, all the untimely mistakes
Swept away with the flames, the jerry-built houses and stores,

"The monstrous libels on artistic building," the past
Cancelled and destroyed at last, the country making way
For fireproof commercial buildings anchored in mud.
Who couldn't admire the strength of the underlying steel

Frame, the bones that carried tall buildings into heaven,
The idea that form followed function in a shell of offices
Surrounding a hotel with an L-shaped honeycomb of rooms
And a theater with elliptical arched trusses and perfect
Acoustics, a stage supported on a laminated floor?
On the gala opening night, the Apollo Club sang
A cantata composed by Frederick Grant Gleason,

And the prima donna, Adelina Patti, sang "Home Sweet Home"
To five-thousand cheering citizens. The future
Was still a possibility then—innocent, limitless, free—
And a city was about to be raised into the empty sky.
Think of it: the second idea was a tall office building
Artistically considered at the end of the Nineteenth Century.
The first idea was man walking through space in a tower.

Yellow Light

One arm hooked around the frayed strap
of a tar-black patent-leather purse,
the other cradling something for dinner:
fresh bunches of spinach from J-Town *yaoya,*
sides of split Spanish mackerel from Alviso's,
maybe a loaf of Langendorf; she steps
off the hissing bus at Olympic and Fig,
begins the three-block climb up the hill,
passing gangs of schoolboys playing war,
Japs against Japs, Chicanas chalking sidewalks
with the holy double-yoked crosses of hopscotch,
and the Korean grocer's wife out for a stroll
around this neighborhood of Hawaiian apartments
just starting to steam with cooking
and the anger of young couples coming home
from work, yelling at kids, flicking on
TV sets for the Wednesday Night Fights.

If it were May, hydrangeas and jacaranda
flowers in the streetside trees would be
blooming through the smog of late spring.
Wisteria in Masuda's front yard would be
shaking out the long tresses of its purple hair.
Maybe mosquitoes, moths, a few orange butterflies
settling on the lattice of monkey flowers
tangled in chain-link fences by the trash.

But this is October, and Los Angeles
seethes like a billboard under twilight.
From used-car lots and the movie houses uptown,
long silver sticks of light probe the sky.
From the Miracle Mile, whole freeways away,

a brilliant fluorescence breaks out
and makes war with the dim squares
of yellow kitchen light winking on
in all the side streets of the Barrio.

She climbs up the two flights of flagstone
stairs to 201-B, the spikes of her high heels
clicking like kitchen knives on a cutting board,
props the groceries against the door,
fishes through memo pads, a compact,
empty packs of chewing gum, and finds her keys.

The moon then, cruising from behind
a screen of eucalyptus across the street,
covers everything, everything in sight,
in a heavy light like yellow onions.

The Underworld

Under the cone of flurried light
blued with cigarette smoke,
we sat in the false, morphined shade
of L.A.'s old Orpheum,
a once lavish Fox now gone to skinflicks,
horror fests and community matinees,
laughing at the silliness on-screen—
two comics, a black and a Jew,
both Afroed and dressed in chicken outfits,
trying to rob a suburban bank.
The black housewives around us
laughed too, nursing and cooing
at their infants who bawled
during the lulls and gunfight scenes,
shushing their older ones
who jounced in their seats, miming
the robot-dance or tossing popcorn, bored.
A few rows up from us was a stagpile
of the unemployed, bachelors in their twenties,
middle-aged fathers graying in cigar smoke,
all of them dressed in satins and polyesters
softly gleaming in the spill-light from the screen.
There was one in particular—a ghetto blade
in green velours—he wore a purple hat too,
and its feather, a peacock's unblinking eye,
bounced and darted, faintly luminous in the dark.
He cackled through the escape and arrest scenes,
calling out to his partners
phrases I couldn't quite make out,
then laughing and muttering deep *Yeahs*
in the rhythm of the talking around him.
I suppose they shared a thrill of recognition,

that old slap five and *I heard that*
from the street corner session,
but something passed among them,
a common pain or delight in, just once,
another's humiliation. It was Monday
or Thursday, and though no rain
was coming down in the streets
outside that I could see,
everybody seemed nonetheless well.
My friend talked about the opulence around us—
coal-black interior walls frescoed
with a chain of demons intertwined,
the stalled parade of aisle and exit lamps
(red grottoes, archipelagoes of colored light)
and plush chairs with their flower-carved fabric
and scalloped backs, the gabled balcony overhead—
everything so ornate and particularized,
designed on a theme of descent
into an irretrievable world—
summer afternoons of phosphates and cowboy serials,
or love made more than potential,
corporeal on-screen, a starlet's hair
undone and almost in your lap, *so real*
that the soul stirred in the body
like a river of cold light sliding
through a forest petrified in winter.

When we left, shuffling out behind
the small crowd lighting up their Kools,
almost embarrassed to be seen
in the harsh house lights, everyone went quiet
from the dissonance of our being there.

We stepped outside to the chill blast
of the low desert turning to fall,
city buses hissing and squeaking by,
slurs of Spanish and disco and rap,
a cop's traffic whistle, a street vendor's call,

the day's last, feeble light
streaked in the eyes, fuzzy Giotto halos
like the stiff, polyester hats
on the shimmering, mingled throngs of the poor.

Garrett Hongo

The Legend

In Memory of Jay Kashiwamura

In Chicago, it is snowing softly
and a man has just done his wash for the week.
He steps into the twilight of early evening,
carrying a wrinkled shopping bag
full of neatly folded clothes,
and, for a moment, enjoys
the feel of warm laundry and crinkled paper,
flannellike against his gloveless hands.
There's a Rembrandt glow on his face,
a triangle of orange in the hollow of his cheek
as a last flash of sunset
blazes the storefronts and lit windows of the street.

He is Asian, Thai or Vietnamese,
and very skinny, dressed as one of the poor
in rumpled suit pants and a plaid mackinaw,
dingy and too large.
He negotiates the slick of ice
on the sidewalk by his car,
opens the Fairlane's back door,
leans to place the laundry in,
and turns, for an instant,
toward the flurry of footsteps
and cries of pedestrians
as a boy—that's all he was—
backs from the corner package store
shooting a pistol, firing it,
once, at the dumbfounded man
who falls forward,
grabbing at his chest.

A few sounds escape from his mouth,
a babbling no one understands
as people surround him
bewildered at his speech.
The noises he makes are nothing to them.
The boy has gone, lost
in the light array of foot traffic
dappling the snow with fresh prints.

Tonight, I read about Descartes'
grand courage to doubt everything
except his own miraculous existence
and I feel so distinct
from the wounded man lying on the concrete
I am ashamed.

Let the night sky cover him as he dies.
Let the weaver girl cross the bridge of heaven
and take up his cold hands.

Richard Howard

Among the Missing

Know me? I am the ghost of Gansevoort Pier.
    Out of the Trucks, beside the garbage scow
    where rotten pilings form a sort of prow,
I loom, your practiced shadow, waiting here

for celebrants who cease to come my way,
    though mine were limbs as versatile as theirs
    and eyes as vagrant. Odd that no one cares
to ogle me now where I, as ever, lay

myself out, all my assets and then some,
    weather permitting. Is my voice so faint?
    Can't you hear me over the river's complaint?
Too dark to see me? Have you all become

ghosts? What earthly good is that? I want
    incarnate lovers hungry for my parts,
    longing hands and long-since lonely hearts!
It is your living bodies I must haunt,

and while the Hudson hauls it burdens past,
    having no hosts to welcome or repel
    disclosures of the kind I do so well,
I with the other ghosts am laid at last.

Fiat Lux

Static from the radio stippled grey as anesthesia dream,
band after band of voices,
the luminous bar or speedometer, column shift. Cruising,
the long battered car fogged
in whiskey breath, the sumptuous trash, canvas scraps, pasteled
bills of lading. Father and daughter—

and over them blue spruce laden with snow arcing the white
mansioned avenue of robber barons'
palaces, the steamship magnates and celebrities, the city's
skyline gothamed electric
across the horizon. Small hands on the pane wick the chill
until I'm icy pure flame,

outside the big houses, streets unwinding below like a tulle scarf
from a woman's shoulders
to the damp wooden houses huddled in their steam, the marshes'
smoking blackness beyond. Swallow the moon like a coin,
an ivory poker chip polished

for luck, driving fast past the opera singer's house, his name
like nervous laughter, that
music blown to shards, arias of ice, and always the city's
dragon-back silhouette, someplace
a child might never get to. *Fiat lux,* the windows'
glow, buttery and old.

The city's become a figure for the way you've learned to love
what's distant, fantastic,
an abyss of space between. One of those returning things, skeins
of planetary days, lunar phases,
solar years turning harmonies celestial in the blood. One's
never done with the past.

Close your eyes. The laden winter night, hill tumbling down
and beneath the burning meadows'
spreading stain, the runaway's smoking train through roots,
   the blind
white worms and rat swarms
underneath the mercury-colored river. I always loved stories
that began that way: the elaborate entry

to the city of cast-iron garlands and window displays intricate
as a universe with shining cogs
and wheels, a world where night reversed to day, and
   towering women
waterfalled their dynel tresses
in the shelter of marquees, boas spitting plumage in the faces
of nightwaiters.

Yes, the gilded birds, plunder in the turrets. And the pulse,
the mission, secret formulas
discovered all around me, the daughter swept in her black serge
dust-bin coat, tangled in foxtails,
glass eyes, shoplifter's pockets sewn inside stuffed with
   broken trinkets,
cancelled stamps from Peru and Mozambique.

Fingers tracing the skyline through the windshield of that
   battered car:
mere *fiat lux,* tricks,
delusions of sleek verb, the lustrous nouns. How to imagine
those places where chaos
holds sway, the old night where you hear scared laughter pierce
the anesthesia dream, song

of shoulders pushed rough to alley walls, torn caress, dark dress,
song that goes
I'll do it for 10, for 5, I'll do it, burnt spoon twisted in the pocket.
Don't tell her. Child stroking
the frosted pane, galactic, impervious and caught in this endless
coming to be that's endlessly undone,

the long car's weaving tracks blurred quickly in the snow beneath
the laden shelter of trees,
my father's whiskied breath as we drove like thieves through
   skeins
of planetary nights, air rich
with signals, the arias and perfect boundless schemes where
the city floated
distant and celestial, brutal in its own rung music.

The Time #2

(For North Philly)

I do know this:
Somebody must've dropped the bomb
Yet they say no war has been fought here

Grasses grow in the city streets
and fireflies come in swarms this summer
flowing fluorescently sharp
lighting on the heads of infants
Everything out of order
—the slow drift of mangled cars
—the stillness of mangled bodies
has become order.

They say no war has been fought here
but the eyes of dead slumping buildings
are invaded by irreverent birds
and my head floats five feet over my neck
in the distant city
with the green bitch in the harbor.

And we lay homeless with hollow eyes
among the high-tech rubble
at the mouth of fouled rivers
at the ends of alleys, near railroad tracks
in the path of quickly advancing troops.

But no.
There are no soldiers
and they say no war has been fought here.

It's just another Buddha-belly
coming to collect the rent
It's just the mice in the walls
trapped and singing like Michael Jackson
starving cheerleaders,
poisoned, dying
singing death songs.

Whatever they say, I do know this:
Here in this chamber, in the bowels
of the city, in the flat stench of Sharpeville
in the villages of Haiti,
they split you side to side
with pretty-pretty bayonets.
The tiny blood vessels never link hands again.
And your rivers
never run
quite like before.

Mark Jarman

Los Angeles

for David Myers

In that city we were perfect
citizens, good boys
and punks with car keys.
Though you the defiant Jew
and I the preacher's kid,
on freeways high and smooth
as altar tops, the wheel
spun that difference into haze.
Driving, clutching at a host
of girlfriends, we both
learned the thrill of God was in our hands.

White by night, like letters, floodlit,
stamped on green enamel,
our purity seemed certain.
The signs we looked for said,
this is your entrance, is your exit.
In the garden of high speed,
over rain slick and spilled oil
we flowed with the flow of traffic;
the sacred flares spurted fire;
the banks of iceplant and the ivy fences,
gouged by accidents, flew past.

The luck that did not let
the low, yellow sky collapse
our lungs, that got us home past
midnight at 60 miles per hour
we blessed
for giving us tongues, white skin,

fingers with sensitive tips,
and minds that could doze to loud music
or swell with their own sexual hum
as we drove, with one hand in a pocket,
or lay in bed, legs stroked apart.

If you dreamed of Moses wearing
that sky like a skull cap
or I just as clearly saw Jesus
nailed to a blacktop,
they were visions kept secret,
fulfilling somehow, but nothing
to wish for. We wanted girls.
Let them be wicked cheerleaders.
Let them be Mother. We wanted
dreams of girls, real girls
we could put in the car.

We prayed to the engines,
we prayed to the driveways,
to the layers of oil, those belts
of black on the gray streets
our parents paid for, we prayed
to the fumes of gasoline
in our membranes: Give us
girls with flammable skin.
Let our fingers for just one evening
be like lit matches
and not break into sweat.

We learned that prayer only
put us to sleep. We awoke
with our own hands drowned
in ourselves; the intricate resolutions
to drive until satisfied
ground down like slipped gears.
Though at times we persuaded skin

to rub our skin and felt almost
the perfect fit,
as the sparks flew upwards,
we were virgins spinning our wheels.

We were tanks to be filled
with any cheap, glorious promise.
When self-pity burned out
we pumped ourselves full
of holy convictions: there was always
sainthood, always the car,
always the usual solace:
We could have been young blacks
growing up to brace
our hips by the roadside, shoveling
crushed glass into oil drums.

My God, we could have been girls,
approached by hands like ours,
becoming mothers driving for children.
With the greased pedal underfoot,
we roared our self-satisfaction
to the mountains and highrises
bulging through haze,
the concrete's field of heat waves,
the thick film of sunlight
on the Pacific, the earth
that smelled good as fresh gas.

All along, the small revelations
of loss splattered our vision,
and far ahead in the dark
a drop of blood-light
seemed to touch some figure
that we knew. But we kept
hunting, sure that with chrome,
upholstery, plastic, the stock
accessories of praise,

we'd find the place a fingertip
could nestle, not abuse.

What you found and I found
for the hands that held the wheel
and tinkered with crosses, prayer cloths,
and sweated on girls' knees,
was the city suddenly
out of reach; the city like a model
of our past, under glass.
At times, we kneel before it,
worshipping our lives there.
At times, we hover over, knowing,
helpless, looking on.

Mark Jarman

The Homing Instinct

There we see him, driving
the canyon's winding stem,
   from sea marsh
    through sweet real estate,
late in the afternoon.

   A huge doll
   frocked in yellow
sits beside him on the seat.
Her eyes rock open and look
   through cellophane.

She is a gift for Madame Ling
who sits beside the stage
   after the Island dancing
   in her restaurant
and lets the young bands play.

   The light peels
   from eucalyptus trees
and clusters in chaparral.
And suddenly a cloud of bees,
   dancing for a queen,

gilds the air. It rides
his radio's thumping pulse,
   a crazy rain
   of loyalty,
each note a little fury.

Windows up,
  safe as the doll's
hard and rosy skin,
he nods in time to this music,
  and then it dies.

When he enters Madame Ling's,
strobed by the harsh silver
  as the bass begins,
  he will call for her
and try to catch her eye.

  Meanwhile the day
  recedes, and where
the canyon rises among
the freeways, he enters night.
  We see him there,

his face patched by passing lights,
his neck and shoulders thrusting
  back and forth
  to another beat
we faintly hear. We see him.

  We see the city
  let him take
its privacy, like a nectar,
and mix it with his nerves,
  and make it honey.

Patricia Spears Jones

Christmas, Boston 1989

This is how I know God exists:
God made cold.

God made sky the color of milk
God lets children eat their breath.

At the corner of the plaza, women in expensive coats
praise God's name. JESUS, they shout.

Jesus slaps back.
Wind on cheek. Every tremble a sign.

At twilight, his most faithful servants
present oblations: wine bottles, beer cans,

half-eaten donuts, orange rinds, banana skins,
cups and cups of black sugarless coffee.

Couples dance across icy streets glad
to get from one side to the other.

Left behind are winter gifts:
gloves, socks, boots, brassieres.

Across the parched milky sky,
electric lights bloom.

Patricia Spears Jones

Day of the Dead

Here is Brooklyn
here are the Anglos
here is the Day of the Dead

This makes sense, what with
all the blood spilled in battles
from Sheepshead Bay to Red Hook

Not even a microscopic mention in the *Times*
unless five or more bats are used
to beat down the young men, mostly
Black, White, Hispanic
English speaking?

So all these well-traveled people have brought back
perfect rituals appropriate really to the desert
and hills of Mexico. But we have our deserts,
our hills. Our bluffs and valleys, too. Our bridges, our tunnels
and those subterranean maps like Escher's etchings—
rational schematics for daily trekking

from island to island
dream to dream.

So dressed in black from head to toe
we walk as if from one funeral to another
from Christian hymns to Buddhist sutras
always in this weather, a casual regard

for the walk from one street to the other
breathing the sugar cube skeletons
happy for the privilege.

Prayer

There are words that refuse me:
hermeneutics, tensile, circadian.

They feel like old expensive furniture
lovingly made for little use.

No, I should have learned them at eighteen
the way I learned to drink cheap wine.

No money again, just the usual dire straits
sharp dry leaves turn cyclone mean
and the full moon already gone.

Halloween weather, words of no use—
A mirror on the war within or just a popular song.

A tall poor black man fiercely holds his elaborate CD player
as it outblasts all the obscenities on Vanderbilt Avenue.

And I know every one of them
by heart.

Down on my knees or down on my luck.
Lord, oh lord, deliver me.

Romance of the Poor

The poor people in Springfield go to Dayton to be miserable
    in style.
They can hug themselves when they lie side by side on the
    iron cots.
They can luxuriate in one red bean held under the tongue.
For them, a discarded refrigerator crate, tipped on its side
    and lined with plastic bags,
Is the green shore of an island and a palace's velvet halls.
Every morning they check out of the Club St. Vincent de Paul,
And they clump in the warm gusts that scowl up from the sewers.

They can strip the aluminum from gutters as their mothers
    harvested eggs from boxes of straw.
Against that snow that is all edge, they can wobble and career
    from bumper to lightpole,
Dancing with the parking meter before dying into the hydrant
    under the fire escape.
Deliriously happy, they lift the sweetest and heaviest wine
    and sink down where the metal is warm,
Across from the cafeteria and that other richest trough,
Kingdom of heaven on earth, emerald dumpster of the pizzeria

What does it matter if I heap treasure from the stick people,
    far off and helpless, fluttering of brown coats?
Their lives are not my life. I come as a tourist to their woe.
But I remember how quickly dark fell, twenty years ago, thumbing
    from Greensboro to Boulder.
I carried one change of clothes, a notebook, and a little more
    than seven dollars.
And I thought I could live by the grace of hippies and priests
    or, failing that,
Prey on park squirrels and the ducks from municipal ponds.

I did not have to go that way. I could have gone on wrestling
    those big sacks of fertilizer
From the co-op's storage bins to the beds of pickup trucks,
Or bludgeoning ice from the front steps of the coliseum,
But I had to get it straight from the black road and the mouth
    of the blue norther.
There is a high ledge under every overpass where you can sleep
    if it is not too cold.
One morning I woke there beside a short man, a carnie and ex-con
    reared
In the Tennessee Industrial School and a dozen foster homes.

We talked a stupid dream of burglary. We committed the crime
    of brotherhood.
Then, hungry and stiff, we trudged up the ramp to a truckstop,
    where he meant
To convince me to knife a man for three hundred dollars
    locked in a drawer.
He said we could get away, we could take any one of those semis
    idling outside that place
Like great buffaloes blowing clouds and clearing their throats.
But I have taken small. I have gotten away clean to Illinois.

Tonight the steaks frown up at me through the odor of blood,
And the poor need no help from poems to limp down the alley
    and up into the van.
They glide to Dayton. They check in to the Club St. Vincent
    de Paul.
Whatever it is, it is not much that makes a man more
    than a scrap of paper
Torn out of a notebook and thrown from the window of a bus,
    but it is more than nothing.
If he holds himself straight up and does not take the life
Next to his own, give him that much. Leave him to his joy.

Rodney Jones

Progress Alley

How did I miss this isthmus of old bricks between the Shelter-
Workshop and the Dominion Bank,
This bumpy lane, not even a street now, but pot-holed and tar-
streaked, and smeared with the indiscriminate droppings of
pigeons?
In the seventies, these were the blocks I loved, squat little downtown,
its Roxy closed
And boarded up, the domed theater dark and mattress-strewn,
a few drunks sleeping it off there
In the place of dreams, with the spidery stars of a faded velvet
heaven falling into their beards.
I stood outside that place one afternoon, vagrant beneath the random
lettering of the broken marquee.
I was not in that much trouble. Why did I turn then and look so
closely?

Except for the first mountains to the east, which, in March,
were still purple-brown and crested with snow,
Everything was used up, rusted or sere, warped on winter's flinty
edge—just left there—
Buildings and men, and I loved them for their cracked faces
and greasy food.
I took each rip and splinter as Baudelaire took his cripples
and imbeciles,
As the true pessimist relishes the catastrophe that comfirms his
faith.
Let Baptists roll in mountain rivers, shouting hosannahs to their
holy ghost. More than the mountains,
I loved that majorette in pink cowgirl fringe as she sank with her
1940's cola into the acid of the concrete wall behind the
hardware.

And more than any flower or shrub, I loved that slattern of
  a broken hotel
Where Jimmie Rodgers once sang of his own loneliness and bitter
  trains.

It took him years. By the time he found his songs, he was dying in
  public and in shame,
And his voice was no river, it was the small sweetness after a long
  briar is plucked from under a nail.
I would not pull him back through the scratch and laceration of the
  needle, his yodel swaying now like the imperfect pirouette of a
  skater.
The engines are gone that towed his boxcars out of the coalfields.
Refashioned as a mall, his depot catches in a dull web of
  suspended tracks, and Rodgers is no ghost
To guide me through the side-alleys of poolhalls and pawnshops,
  to stand with me on State Street,
Both of us loathing the city's sandblasted bricks, the newly
  installed dogwoods
That are blossoming already in their tended circles of salt-treated
  boards.

Most of my country abhors filth and denounces a ruin, but I want
  that heart that ripens in desolation.
Not the showy glass of cathedrals, but the bent poles under
  a sagging awning.
I stand across from the drygoods and the jewelry stores, dreaming
  of brothels,
And I wait awhile on the wrought-iron bench in front of the
  smashed saloon where the heavy matriarchs went hushing the
  fiddles.
A ghost loves a low place where the street sinks through a broken
  drain and finds in a pool of oil
Under a rusting Cadillac the last ripple in the long-lingering odor
  of horses.
Daily, he assumes the untunable shape. He escapes the longing
  for perfection.

If I must sing at all of renewal, let me gather a choir from all the losses. I will laugh again with
The left-handed spirits. I will dance in this sacred alley of the Protestants.

Lawrence Joseph

There I Am Again

I see it again, at dusk, half darkness in its brown light,
large tenements with pillars on Hendrie beside it,

the gas station and garage on John R beside it,
sounds of acappella from a window somewhere, pure, nearby it

pouring through the smell of fried pork to welcome
whoever enters it to do business.

Today, again, in the second year of the fifth recession
my father holds pickled feets, stomachs and hearts,

I lift crates of okra and cabbages,
let down crates of buttermilk and beer,

bring live carp to the scale and come, at last, to respect
the intelligence of roaches in barrels of bottles,

I sell the blood on the wooden floor after the robbery,
salt pork and mustard greens and Silver Satin wine,

but only if you pay, down, on the counter
money you swear you'll never hand over, only if,

for collateral, you don't forget you too may have to kill.
Today, again, in the third year of unlimited prosperity,

the Sunday night the city burns
I hear sirens, I hear broken glass, I believe

the shadow of my father's hand that touches my hair,
my cousin loading a carbine, my uncle losing his mind

today in a place the length of a pig's snout
in a time the depth of a cow's brain

in Joseph's Market on the corner of John R and Hendrie
there I am again: always, everywhere,

apron on, alone behind the cash register, the grocer's son
angry, ashamed, and proud as the poor with whom he deals.

Sand Nigger

In the house in Detroit
in a room of shadows
when grandma reads her Arabic newspaper
it is difficult for me to follow her
word by word from right to left
and I do not understand
why she smiles about the Jews
who won't do business in Beirut
"because the Lebanese
are more Jew than Jew,"
or whether to believe her
that if I pray
to the holy card of Our Lady of Lebanon
I will share the miracle.
Lebanon is everywhere
in the house: in the kitchen
of steaming pots, leg of lamb
in the oven, plates of kousa,
hushwee rolled in cabbage,
dishes of olives, tomatoes, onions,
roasted chicken, and sweets;
at the card table in the sunroom
where grandpa teaches me
to wish the dice across the backgammon board
to the number I want;
Lebanon of mountains and sea,
of pine and almond trees,
of cedars in the service
of Solomon, Lebanon
of Babylonians, Phoenicians, Arabs, Turks
and Byzantines, of the one-eyed
monk, Saint Maron,

in whose rite I am baptized;
Lebanon of my mother
warning my father not to let
the children hear,
of my brother who hears
and from whose silence
I know there is something
I will never know; Lebanon
of grandpa giving me my first coin
secretly, secretly
holding my face in his hands,
kissing me and promising me
the whole world.
My father's vocal cords bleed;
he shouts too much
at his brother, his partner
in the grocery store that fails.
I hide money in my drawer, I have
the talent to make myself heard.
I am admonished to learn,
never to dirty my hands
with sawdust and meat.
At dinner, a cousin
describes his niece's head
severed with bullets, in Beirut,
in civil war. "More than
an eye for an eye," he demands,
breaks down, and cries.
My uncle tells me to recognize
my duty, to use my mind,
to bargain, to succeed.
He turns the diamond ring
on his finger, asks if
I know what asbestosis is,
"the lungs become like this,"
he says, holding up a fist;
he is proud to practice
law which "distributes

money to compensate flesh."
Outside the house my practice
is not to respond to remarks
about my nose or the color of my skin.
"Sand nigger," I'm called,
and the name fits: I am
the light-skinned nigger
with black eyes and the look
difficult to figure—a look
of indifference, a look to kill—
a Levantine nigger
in the city on the strait
between the great lakes Erie and St. Clair
which has a reputation
for violence, an enthusiastically
bad-tempered sand nigger
who waves his hands, nice enough
to pass, Lebanese enough
to be against his brother,
with his brother against his cousin,
with cousin and brother
against the stranger.

Lawrence Joseph

Do What You Can

In the Church of I AM she hears there is a time to heal,
but her son, Top Dog of the Errol Flynn gang,

doesn't lay down his sawed-off shotgun,
the corn she planted in the field where

the Marvel Motor Car factory once was
doesn't grow with pigweed and cockleburr.

When someone in the Resurrection Lounge laughs,
"Bohunk put the 2-foot dogfish in the whore's hand,"

someone's daughter whispers, "Fuck you,"
places a half-smoked cigarette in her coat pocket,

swings open the thick wooden door and walks
into air that freezes when it hears frost

coming from Sault Sainte Marie. Driving, I see
a shed of homing pigeons, get out of my car to look.

I answer, "What you care?" to a woman who shouts, "What you
    want?"
Beside the Church of St. John Nepomocene

an old man, hunched and cold, prays, "Mother of God"
to a statue of the Virgin Mary

surrounded by a heart-shaped rosary
of 53 black and 6 white bowling balls.

Where the Ford and Chrysler freeways cross
a sign snaps, 5,142,250,

the number of cars produced so far this year in America.
Not far away, on Beaufait Street,

a crowd gathers to look at the steam
from blood spread on the ice. The light red,

I press the accelerator to keep the motor warm.
I wonder if they know

that after the jury is instructed
on the Burden of Persuasion and the Burden of Truth,

that after the sentence of 20 to 30 years comes down,
when the accused begs, "Lord, I can't do that kind of time,"

the judge, looking down, will smile and say,
"Then do what you can."

A Taxi to the Flame

Halloween, I ride the subway to an early evening class
On poetry and the subconscious.

Beneath unearthly light, a man dressed as a skull and bones
Stares into the near reaches of the civilized underworld.

You would have liked the way
He politely let the living on first.

The empty seats take on a pumpkin glow, whipped
By hairs of electricity, as we shoot along at witch's speed.

A girl with a spider on her cheek reads the *Times*.
Where are we exactly?

Below 23rd. Below 14th. Below
The flat-footed beat cops and the swift commuters.

At the turn of the century, tunneling a subway
Under Boston Common, blasters uncovered shells, tools,

Even graves—an entire lateral town.
Trees, like repressed thoughts,

Were lifted out and regraded when found to be
Inconveniently deep.

A world spread its fingers under us and lifted us
Up, up by putting so much imagination beneath.

Look, I will tell my class, at the patterns in the wood
Of your desk and write down what you see:

Church spires crowded one upon the next in flat daylight,
A chorus of architecture pressed, as if into a book, of wood.

Now think of someone you've lost, someone you miss,
And tell that person about it.

I think of you and that time we took a cab to the East River Drive
To watch the Burns Brothers factory burn down.

We saw no people. No brothers. Just burning.
And behind it, a sunset repeating the pattern.

What I remember best were the clear delineations:
The sad wobbly factory all dark and ash and lit with borrowed
    menace;

The sky an anthology of color with no preface or ending,
No intention of serving as a symbol of anything.

But years later, lit by the context of your death,
I wonder about the Burns brothers.

Were they inside? Were they insured?
Did they set the fire?

And where, in tonight's sunset,
Is the piece of that flame?

Vickie Karp

The Consequences of Waking

From a fish store window, on their deathbed of ice,
A school of porgies, butterfish and smelts
Considers an elderly stroller holding a bag of shrimp.

In the layering dark, all the shops around him form a sequence
On human evolution. In the pet shop, snakes plunder
The depths of biblical fig trees.

At the dress shop, a bearded tailor clothes a human form
And sticks it, endlessly, with pins. Gloves, on sale,
Hang from invisible wire in a blue diorama,

Lit from underneath like a failed plan for stars.
Gloves point west, mittens thumb rides and palm for change,
But this the tailor doesn't see,

Not the tableau across the street of a pale floor manager
At the *Catch A Wink Bed Boutique* who stands between curtain
    and glass,
Sales pad in hand, watching the moon float.

Mattress salesmen play cards behind the grave-sized bedding
Below a reproduction of Giotto's Lazarus, who is slowly coming to,
On a calendar for MARCH.

Taking the name of the month literally now, they file out together
For the health club pool only to find a bored lifeguard, dozing on
    the diving board
Over a blue-green void.

Lined up now, annoyed, on perhaps the tiniest launch in their
    universe,
They bellow a schoolboy threat, catapault forwards, and jump
Into the still-life of water below.

Later, when they put on their pants and shirts and go,
They pass the fish store filled with expert swimmers
And study, as if shopping out a dream.

The silk parachutes of squid, the recluse clams,
Fifty soiled ballet slippers of sole in a heap,
A whole flounder wrapped round its precious fillet, and,

Closest to the exit, rainbow trout examining the snow
That falls like bait, like a hundred vowels
In search of a language.

Vickie Karp

Still-Life in the Coat Factory Office

for Rosalie Dym

What did you think would happen
When you got on that pale boat and

Came to America, came here to Essex Street,
Where the vibrant machinery of your heart

Is rustic compared to the hiss and boom
Of this captainless ship?

You speak to women you've never met
On the telephone, voices full of curls

And twangs thickened by the borderless
Hallucinations of long-distance wires.

Their laughter clicks and drones until
The women themselves become nothing

But another machine you've learned how to run,
A switchboard for the bodiless voices of Georgia.

In the beginning, they squealed at
Your accent and you clucked at theirs.

You've made up a game about it—you
Pretend it's all French and elegant as lace.

A still-life of the Cafe de la Paix
Hangs by one nail behind the Big Boss' desk.

In the perpetual rain, a woman sits
And stares at her leg.

She doesn't see the broad-chested waiter
Under the awning, but you do.

His face is a lunacy of fixed points
Painstakingly arranged in the name of art.

He's been looking straight at you for years,
Waiting to take your order.

Natural History

The jewelers' windows have been muted with
black felt, their crystal riot locked away
for one more night. And yet, so profligate,
so close-set is their unrelenting blaze,
that, after dark, imagination brings
it's own combustion, worn to one blood-red
cabochon by the friction of its passage.

How many hands are worn away with toil
so that a single knuckle shines resplendent?
Silica dust sharpens and clouds the air
from somewhere high above, like snow wind-driven
across a pristine landscape of spruce tips.
But in the risky sandstone vineyards and
arbors of pomegranate finials

five storeys up, there are two midway angels
whose only thoughts are barnacled with earth.
They bring a local weather with them (rain),
although the blinking sign above them reads
AUGUST FIFTH 10:00 PM TOMORROW: FAIR.
Their oilskins whicker as they shift along
the narrow scaffold, and their arc lamps veer

madly. Their backs are to the world of sense.
They mix the common sand with water struck
from the brass bole of a standpipe. Their hands
are turned against the vegetable stone,
which holds no ransom for them anymore.
They are trying to drive their shadows from the wall.
By dawn, with filthy tears, they will succeed.

Karl Kirchwey

Rogue Hydrant, August

Morning. The sun gleams wickedly on chrome:
neuralgic intimations for the day.
Up from those stone vaults where the boiler men
in beaked quartz masks wield their erratic torches
on mudlegs, coils and firebrick, erupts
this vengeful glossolalia, to scour
a rank pot liquor from the granite curb
(turds, chewing gum, butts, sputum, wilted flowers),
led from upstate through locomotive-sized
conduits, with the thumb of gravity
pressing and pressing on a glassy core.

A wino from the traffic island puts
insouciant lips down to the furious stream
(two hundred p.s.i., through ductile iron),
his thirst, for once, not dropsical enough
to quench the music of this braided storm.
Oh to lie down, he thinks, and feed upon
this foggy clout and, as at some old loom,
study the gauzy cadence of release,
weaving itself forever fresh and new,
cross-rhymed, flashing high and low (just like
that nearby boxtop game of three-card monte):

I *will* lead me beside stiller waters than these,
where chance is pastured greenly—and swoons closer.
Too close! It rolls him off, with crystal knives
break-dancing all around. But, for one instant,
he's balanced on the cusp of pleasure's tooth,
buried a hundred years beneath the pavement;
then grovels back through oscillating rings
of perfect clarity, through chlorinated

precincts of freshness, to the muggy street.
He wakes, stands, and vaguely wanders away
just as the water-blue squad car arrives.

Ambulance

The caduceus flies past, with serpents wrought
And wings, with clever reversed lettering
For mirror-reading. Feel your own heart beat,
    Sped by this urgent pacing,

Outrider in oncoming lanes of traffic,
An ululation on the already-
Violated air, a passing bell to make
    This brief hysteria,

And lights that positively bulge and loll
In celebration, as if the collapse
Of one life were a public festival.
    The city stands and gapes,

Asking the subject of that roaring tableau,
That hurled interior like a mundane
Pietà seen for a moment through a window:
    Figures stooped over someone,

It could be you, luxuriously watching. Here is what
Happened: a coronary on the sidewalk.
She sprawls, a fruitstand pyramid of pomegranate
    Around her head. She took

Them down with her, and now the bitter rind
And sweet bloodblossom of each misty cell
Have made a salad for her fading mind,
    A lapsarian rubble.

A laborer, whose spattered galoshes
Just now flung globs of green concrete around

As he strode like a diver toward what pressures
    And sheer pH had found

And ruptured like a valve deep in a salt mine
Kneels, pumps, shouts, "Give her air!"; who was
            off-work,
Careless a moment past, like everyone
    Who gathers now to look;

His body buoyant as it would be (hands
Tied behind) once cast into the Dead Sea:
Sudden, blown upward as if by strong winds.
    Fighting that buoyancy,

The circle closes, calculating, as
When vendors on streetcorners sell some hot
Item: a ring of concentrating stares
    Past the anonymity of feet

Till that brief concrete stage is all that remains
Of the surprising drama that is price:
Watches forgotten, Walkmans, or keychains
    That respond to a human voice.

August Kleinzahler

San Francisco/New York

A red band of light stretches across the west,
low over the sea, as we say good-bye to our friend,
Saturday night, in the room he always keeps unlit
and head off to take in the avenues,
actually take them in, letting the gables,

bay windows and facades impress themselves,
the clay of our brows accepting the forms.
Darkness falls over the district's slow life,
miles of pastel stucco canceled
with its arched doorways and second floor businesses:

herbalists and accountants, jars
of depilatories. Such a strange calm, the days
lengthening and asparagus already
under two dollars a pound.
                              Is New York fierce?

The wind, I mean. I dream of you in the shadows,
hurt, whimpering. But it's not like that, really,
is it? lots of taxis and brittle fun.
We pass the shop of used mystery books
with its ferrety customers and proprietress

behind her desk, a swollen arachnid
surrounded by murder and the dried-out glue
of old paperback bindings.
                              What is more touching
than a used bookstore on Saturday night,

dowdy clientele haunting the aisles:
the girl with bad skin, the man with a tic,

some chronic ass at the counter giving his art speech?
How utterly provincial and doomed we feel
tonight with the streetcar appearing over the rise

and at our backs the moon full in the east,
lighting the slopes of Mt. Diablo
and the charred eucalyptus in the Oakland hills.
Did you see it in the East 60's
or bother to look for it downtown?

And where would you have found it,
shimmering over Bensonhurst, over Jackson Heights?
It fairly booms down on us tonight
with the sky so clear,
                              and through us

as if these were ruins, as if we were ghosts.

East of the Library, Across from the Odd Fellows Building

That bummy smell you meet
off the escalator at Civic Center, right before
you turn onto McAllister,
seems to dwell there, disembodied,
on a shelf above the sidewalk.

The mad old lady with lizard skin
bent double
               over her shopping cart
and trailing a cloud of pigeons
is nowhere in sight.

A pile of rags here and there
but no one underneath.
                     An invisible shrine
commemorating what?
Old mattresses and dusty flesh,

piss and puked-on overcoats, what?
                 Maybe death,
now there's a smell that likes to stick around.
You used to find it in downtown Sally Anns
and once

in a hospital cafeteria, only faintly,
after a bite of poundcake.
                    But here it lives,
cheek by jowl with McDonald's,
still robust after a night of wind

with it own dark little *howdy-do*
for the drunks and cops,

social workers and whores,
or the elderly couple from Zurich
leafing coolly through their guidebook.

Yusef Komunyakaa

The Cage Walker

He shoves the .38
into his coat pocket
& walks back into
the dark. Night
takes him like a conveyer belt.

For a split second
he's been there
in the ditch,
hood pulled from over a death's-head.

He sits on a park bench.
Blue uniform behind every elm,
night sticks. He thinks how a man
enters the deeper, darker machine.

His fingers touch gun metal.
He stands & walks down
toward the wharf; ships rock
in white foghorn silence.
Water slams, steel doors
closing in a tunnel.

The quarter-moon goes blank
behind a cloud. He frames a picture
in his head, retraces his footsteps
to Shorty's Liquor Store.
He will go in this time.

He stands under a street lamp.
Moths float by
& he counts cars:
1, 2, 3, 4, 5, aw shit.

A woman walks past & smiles.
Her red dress turns the corner
like blood in a man's eyes.
He stares at his hands.
They say August is a good time
for a man to go crazy.

Yusef Komunyakaa

Crack

You're more jive than Pigmeat
   & Dolemite, caught by a high note
      stolen from an invisible sax.

I've seen your sequinned nights
   pushed to the ragged end
      of a drainpipe, swollen fat

with losses bitter as wormwood,
   dropped tongues of magnolia
      speaking a dead language.

You're an eyeload, heir
   to cottonfields & the North Star
      balancing on a needle.

Where's the loot, at Scarlett O'Hara's
   or buying guns for the Aryan Nation?
      The last time I saw you,

merchant of chaos, you were beating
   days into your image as South African
      diamonds sparkled in your teeth.

Now, Cain's daughter waits with two minks
   in a tussle around her neck, fastened
      with a gold catch.

You pull her closer, grinning up
   at barred windows, slinky
      as a cheetah on a leash.

You're the Don of Detroit,
   gazing down from your condo
      at the night arranged into a spasm

band, & groupies try to steady their hands
   under an incantation of lights, nailed
      to a dollar sign & blonde wig.

Desire has eaten them from inside:
   the guts gone, oaths lost
      to a dictum of dust

in a dynasty of worms. Hooded
   horsemen out of a Jungian dream
      know you by your mask.

I see ghosts of our ancestors
   clubbing you to the ground.
      Didn't you know you'd be gone,

shaken out like a white sleeve,
   condemned to run down
      a Coltrane riff?

Bullbats sew up the evening
   sky, but there's no one left
      to love you back to earth.

Yusef Komunyakaa

"Everybody's Reading Li Po" Silkscreened on a Purple T-Shirt

Li Po who?
says the shoeless
woman moving toward me with
her faded aura, angry
at no one in this world.

Li Po who?
Murmurs December,
speaking in tongues
like the girl in Jackson Square.
Sweet stench of onion
eats at me as the wind
discovers an old man
asleep under newspapers.
His dream a slow leaf
on black water.

Li Po who?
Says the boy junkie, Ricardo.
Tied to night's string,
he sways under neon
like a black girl with red hair
in the doorway of Lucky's.

Li Po who?
Says the prostitute
on Avenue Z.
Smelling loud as a bag
of lavender sachet
spilled on the sidewalk.
Blue-veined pallor,

she lifts her skirt to show
what a diamond-studded
garter looks like.

David Lehman

Arrival at Kennedy

Reduce the supply while the demand stays constant and the
    result is
No taxis for anybody. Reddening sky, the threat of rain, my
    cabbie's demented laugh
As he lights up a joint & news of Jackie Gleason's death
    comes on the radio.
This is my city, I know that now, though I recognize hardly
    any of the streets.
I'm three drinks ahead of the rest of the cast & trying hard
    to keep my eyes
On Eurydice in the rear-view mirror, who tells me I've arrived,
    welcomes me home,
And warns me to focus on the road ahead. I'd rather have my
    arms around you,
Dear, in the backseat of heaven. Meanwhile, a siren goes off
    in front of the old
Neighborhood hardware store, where a sailor and his girl kissed
    under the awning
And became our parents during World War II. We pass them in
    the cab & feel
Nostalgic for the city before we were born: big band music,
    Rita Hayworth,
Gray fedoras, and the Third Avenue El. In the end, of course,
    we forget why we came,
What brought us together in the lovely humid August night we
    thought would never end
When freedom meant driving a car over a cliff & jumping out
    at the last possible moment.

David Lehman

The Moment of Truth

The pure poetry of paranoia was his as he emerged
From the movie house to find that the film was continuing
In the street and among the musicians on the subway platform
Where a woman with a single dollar bill in her wallet
Fell to her death, trying to resist her assailant. The moment
Of panic: he had entered the theatre with his wife and now
Where was she? How could he have lost her? Alone he relished
The moment of seeing himself on the screen
Courting her, ignoring the consequences of his reckless wish
To grant her half the wealth in his kingdom. In the next scene,
She disrobes before him, freely and without constraint.
That's not how she saw it, of course. She saw things clearly.
The seduction was over, though the orgasms continued.
She *was* beautiful. But was she maybe just a diversion
Arranged by minor deities to keep him busy while
They prepared some new disaster to spoil his weekend?
He wasn't going to think about it now. He was throwing
Caution to the wind. He was going to give a girl a ring
And he didn't give a damn what anybody thought. It was fate
That beckoned, and he went, laughing and crying
The way children do, freely, with tears far in excess
Of the cause: the die of a board game lost in a grate.

An Ordinary Morning

A man is singing on the bus
coming in from Toledo.
His voice floats over the heads
that bow and sway with each
turn, jolt, and sudden slowing.
A hoarse, quiet voice, it tells
of love that is true, of love
that endures a whole weekend.
The driver answers in a tenor
frayed from cigarettes, coffee,
and original curses thrown
down from his seat of command.
He answers that he has time
on his hands and it's heavy.
O heavy hangs the head, he
improvises, and the man
back in the very last row,
bouncing now on the cobbles
as we bump down the boulevard,
affirms that it is hanging,
yes, and that it is heavy.
This is what I waken to.
One by one my near neighbors
open their watering eyes
and close their mouths to accept
this bright, sung conversation
on the theme of their morning.
The sun enters from a cloud
and shatters the wide windshield
into seventeen distinct shades
of yellow and fire, the brakes

gasp and take hold, and we are
the living, newly arrived
in Detroit, city of dreams,
each on his own black throne.

Philip Levine

Coming Home, *Detroit,* 1968

A winter Tuesday, the city pouring fire,
Ford Rouge sulfurs the sun, Cadillac, Lincoln,
Chevy gray. The fat stacks
of breweries hold their tongues. Rags,
papers, hands, the stems of birches
dirtied with words.

                  Near the freeway
you stop and wonder what came off,
recall the snowstorm where you lost it all,
the wolverine, the northern bear, the wolf
caught out, ice and steel raining
from the foundries in a shower
of human breath. On sleds in the false sun
the new material rests. One brown child
stares and stares into your frozen eyes
until the lights change and you go
forward to work. The charred faces, the eyes
boarded up, the rubble of innards, the cry
of wet smoke hanging in your throat,
the twisted river stopped at the color of iron.
We burn this city every day.

Buying and Selling

All the way across the Bay Bridge I sang
to the cool winds buffeting my Ford,
for I was on my way to a life of buying
untouched drive shafts, universal joints,
perfect bearings so steeped in Cosmoline
they could endure a century and still retain
their purity of functional design, they
could outlast everything until like us
their usefulness became legend and they
were transformed into sculpture. At Benicia
or the Oakland Naval Yard or Alameda
I left the brilliant Western sun behind
to enter the wilderness of warehouses
with one sullen enlisted man as guide.
There under the blinking artificial light
I was allowed to unwrap a single sample,
to hack or saw my way with delicacy
through layer after layer of cardboard,
metallic paper, cloth webbing, wax
as hard as wood until the dulled steel
was revealed beneath. I read, if I could,
the maker's name, letters, numbers,
all of which translated into functions
and values known only to the old moguls
of the great international junk companies
of Chicago, Philadelphia, Brooklyn,
whose young emissary I was. I, who at
twenty had wept publicly in the Dexter-
Davison branch of the public library
over the death of Keats in the Colvin
biography and had prayed like him
to be among the immortals, now lived
at thirty by a code of figures so arcane

they passed from one side of the brain
to the other only in darkness. I, who
at twenty-six had abandoned several careers
in salesmanship—copper kitchenware,
Fuller brushes, American encyclopedias—
from door to unanswered door in the down
and out neighborhoods of Detroit, turning
in my sample cases like a general handing
over his side arms and swagger stick, I
now relayed the new gospels across mountains
and the Great Plains states to my waiting masters.
The news came back: Bid! And we did
and did so in secret. The bids were
awarded, so trucks were dispatched,
Mohawks, Tam O'Shanters, Iroquois.
In new Wellingtons, I stood to one side
while the fork lifts did their work,
entering only at the final moment to pay
both loaders and drivers their pittances
not to steal, to buy at last what could
not be bought. The day was closing down.
Even in California the afternoon skies
must turn from blue to a darker blue
and finally take the color of coal, and stars
—the same or similar ones—hidden so long
above the Chicago River or the IRT
to Brooklyn, emerge stubbornly not in ones
but in pairs, for there is safety in numbers.
Silent, alone, I would stand in the truck's
gray wake feeling something had passed,
was over, complete. The great metal doors
of the loading dock crashed down, and in
the sudden aftermath I inhaled a sadness
stronger than my Lucky Strike, stronger
than the sadness of these hills and valleys
with their secret ponds and streams unknown
even to children, or the sadness of children
themselves, who having been abandoned believe
their parents will return before dark.

Dionisio D. Martínez

Fuego

for Jonathan Aaron

Where this train stops not even the engineer
knows: destination
is God's business and he tends to keep
things to himself.
Think of the Christ in Rio de Janeiro turning

his back
on the continent while he watches over the ocean:
from the foothills
even omnipotence seems limited and flawed. We
talk etymology, jargon,

how brief any word can be. When a smoker in the metro
in Madrid wants
a light, he says *¿Tienes fuego?* He wants to know
if you have fire.
Does he think you carry flames in your fists?

You've been studying
the underground routes, listening to the beautiful
percussion
of steel on steel, the trains leaving and the trains
coming and the late

trains making time between stations. Now and then
a wheel locked
and dragged along the track sets off a spark
and the spark disappears
in mid air. From the Number 7 train—coming

out of the East River
and bound for Flushing—Manhattan is the open
palm of a long
severed hand, dusk a huge flame rising out of it.
The restless

boys from Queens are dreaming of arson at the 52nd
Street station. Let them
dream, let them flick their lighters as if they were
snapping their fingers,
let them be Romeos, let them be Jets for a day.

At the firehouse on 51st,
a man returning from a routine job takes off
his fireproof jacket
and walks away from the light. By the time he reaches
the street

the man has become
invisible except for his t-shirt, which is almost
incandescent. A spark
climbs up the dark to the cigarette in his mouth,
the dark holds the fire's

tenuous glow in the caldron of its callused hands.

Dionisio D. Martínez

A Necessary Story

Take two people. Any two people.
This man of imaginary sorrow,
for instance, and the woman
who follows him everywhere, carrying
his sorrow. Take these two
for the sake of argument,
for the sake of what you've
come to call a necessary story.
He notices the subtleties of dusk,
how grass in winter at this
hour turns from one indescribable
shade to another. He knows
the street well, the spot
where workers spent weeks digging
and repairing and later forgot
to finish the job: now the street
dips at that spot, and the cold
rains gather for days at a time. He
knows every bone in the human foot,
has felt and counted each
one on the walks he has taken
to memorize this street. Now take
the woman. The man concentrates
on the things he can hold.
She, on the other hand, can only
see—and remember, months later,
when they talk about this moment—
how the red and blue lights
on the roof of the tallest building this
side of the river would flash.
After a while she would see
a pattern in this.

And she would follow the pattern
with her eyes. She'd
follow each light until the whole
row flashing on and off created
in her distant eyes the illusion
of movement: the lights seemed
to move, then the entire building,
then the buildings around it
and the sky and the man beside her.
The lights were clear. The movement
of the world was clear. Only
the man beside her remained a blurred
thing, a broken shadow dragging a
man along a street of imaginary sorrow.

Nightscape

It's not only my lights that hum in this city
through the arc of night
at two a.m. when I'm up again, waiting.
There's the lights of the bridge, a disinterested moon,
blue TV glare by the carwash downstairs where
three black men blink into forty-year-old love scenes
and rock in their chairs.
A purple light hangs soft by the river.
In a bright yellow light a mother suckles her child
her head falling over its hungry mouth.
Upstairs a man knocks his wife to the floor,
drunk again, no light in her,
but the heat of their angers spark and fall
to the windows below.
Under nodding streetlights junkies trade, shoot, waste
the   Chinese waiter pees in the lot,
the   taxi driver lights a cigarette, waits for his fare,
the   policeman slams his car door, runs for a beer.
Who is the fireman who masturbates urgently as his wife
        sleeps beside him dreaming of fire,
who curls in his sleep unwilling to wake,
who types unfamiliar names and addresses on envelopes
        calculating
the   chickens and shoes she will buy with the extra cash,
who scrawls in her notebook the dream of a woman to hold
        her,
who holds her new lover imagining his history of fucking,
who fondles his pistol reliving the mother who beat him?
Lovers, destroyers, move through this city through so many
    windows
it seems no one is sleeping.

Vigilant, restless, I chew the cords of my own unravelling
    hungers,
split into a roomful of pictures that shimmer along walls.
I join the ring of rootless insomniacs, trying to chisel a
        shape out of longing,
to say, yes, here is a white bowl on the windowsill, and
        beyond that
the street-echo, and men who sleep under mattress-tents by
        the river
as though night itself were a big house.

Muertes

The event's already happened
Though in another country . . .
The elegies no longer exist
Or are yet to exist if in another life

Over the valley   the news travels
Briefly in eternity   beyond the family . . .
And the shrews know nothing of it
They've the whole sky yet are tiny . . .

A face too can meet the white of the sun
The grief of creation   and be less
Than a pebble   a proverbial mote of dust
In an hourglass   as in AMOR FATI . . .

   In the city
Down by the docks   in the city
The animals hang in consecrated portions
On hooks leading to trucks . . .

If I stroll in the city
Along the pavement of West Street
I can see the carcasses of the flesh stripped and cut
Can smell the blood without name and without pain . . .

At night beneath the skyscrapers
Or the warehouses   the odor's still there
When guilt's aroused and the mourners circle one another
Ready to eat or be eaten

While across the Hudson
Over the plains where no one shall hear them

The burial trains rattle on under the moonlight
Past carousel or foxhole

And in their prisons
The whores and the cons must dream again of ways to feel safe
As once Cervantes in jail
Sought the dream of a windmill . . .

   Now in the city it's noon
As I write   and *no man's an island*
and *each man has his life in his own hands* . . .
But far off from the city   we'll drop

Out of the unknown
Into history   where the heart's a parachute
That'll never fail to open   compact and utterly reliable
It carries us past the babble of heaven

Till we touch earth and the soul is set free

Honolulu

There are quays here
That disappear into the black water
The way the old sailor

Once imagined the world
To split at its farthest point
Lost in the deepest mist . . .

———

Occasionally the people stroll alone
In the moonlight
Bare feet at home in bits of surf

The echoes of black other days
Mingle with the obscure black shapes
Of picnic tables or banyan trees

The outriggers left side by side
On clumps of sand or the surfboards
Kept in strict and measured rows

While the two yachts SHANGRI-LA
And NY NY seem to grope one another
At a boat basin near a parking lot

———

In the lobbies of the dream museums
The carpets wear the designs of jonquil
Sun beasts fathomless roots and maps

At an after hours spot in a "ship's bar"
The porthole or the captain's wheel
Recall no suitable refrain or harbor

———

Yet to resign oneself to what
Is missing or to what is found
Are these the new beginnings

Those galleries of stars that choose
A snowy sky and mountain those spyglasses
Of sleep that meet a distant forest

The three strange figures on a balcony
With the toys piled high in caneback chairs
Or that boy and girl who'll look down now

Past a dim courtyard as an old woman
In plumeria leaves and red chiffon
Waves a farewell and a huge black taxi departs

Robert Mazzocco

PBS

The ferries go out with the bodies from the morgue,
on a cool winter's day, the ferries go out,
carrying off the bodies of strangers, who have been found,
desolate and alone, lost in the heart of the city.

And high in the sky, Canadian geese
follow in the wake of the ferries, eagerly they follow,
as a kind of civic duty, the motley cargo from the morgue,
afloat now on a one way journey over to Potters Field.

And the inmates from nearby Rikers Island
are on burial detail at the island cemetery,
and they labor from nine to five, and wear
stiff woolen caps and black cotton gloves,
as they line up each and every coffin
or dig each and every pit,
as they lower the coffin deep in the ground,
then shovel the dirt high on top of the coffin,
each plot of earth bearing
an appropriate number or a raggedy white streamer,
till the unknown men, women, and children settle down
beneath the sod in the mass graves at Potters Field.

Thousands of these cadavers
keep travelling over from the city
each year on the ferries,
which are like garbage scows,
only it is not garbage they carry,
and high in the sky Canadian geese
follow in the wake of the ferries.

Relatives and friends discover each year
their loved ones buried here . . .

And yet how quiet it is at the island cemetery
once it is twilight and the inmates
from nearby Rikers Island return to Rikers Island,
and not a sound is to be heard,
amid the murmuring sea wind,
except for the daft plaint
of two or three of our vagabond geese,
again and again circling
round the shadow of a cross,
huge, and built on the summit of the island, and made of concrete,
a few traces of a bright snow
whirling about low in the darkening air.

Susan Mitchell

A Story

There is a bar I go to when I'm in Chicago
which is like a bar I used to go to when I lived in New York.
There are the same men racing toy cars
at a back table, the money passing so fast
from hand to hand, I never know who's winning, who's losing,
only in the New York bar the racers sport Hawaiian shirts
while in the Chicago bar they wear Confederate caps
with crossed gold rifles pinned to their bands.
Both bars have oversized TVs and bathrooms
you wouldn't want to be caught dead in,
though some have. Once in the New York bar I watched a film
on psychic surgery, and I swear to you
the surgeon waved a plump hand—
the hand hovered like a dove over the patient's back,
and where wings grow out of an angel's shoulders
a liquid jetted, a clear water, as if pain
were something you could see into like a window.
Later, walking home with a friend
who was also a little drunk, I practiced psychic surgery
on our apartment building, passing my hands
back and forth over the bricks.
I don't know what I expected to happen,
maybe I hoped a pure roach anguish would burst forth.
But there was only the smell that rises out of New York City
in August, a perennial urine—dog, cat, human—
the familiar stench of the body returning to itself as alien.
Sometimes, before stopping in at the Chicago bar,
I would either sleep or go for a walk,
especially in October when the leaves had turned red.
As they swept past me, I thought of my blood
starting to abandon my body,
taking up residence elsewhere like the birds

gathering in feverish groups on the lawns.
In the Chicago bar there were men who never watched TV
or played the video games, mainly from the Plains tribes they
sat in silence over their whiskey, and looking at them,
I could even hear the IRT as it roared through
the long tunnel between Borough Hall and Wall Street,
the screech of darkness on steel.
And it happened one night that a man,
his hair loose to his shoulders, stood up and pulled
a knife from his boot, and another man
who must have been waiting all his life for this
stood up in silence too, and in seconds
one of them was curled around the knife in his chest
as if it were a mystery he would not reveal to anyone.
Sometimes I think my life is what I keep escaping.
Staring at my hands, I almost expect them to turn
into driftwood, bent and polished by the waves,
my only proof I have just returned from a long journey.
The night Tom Littlebird killed Richard Highwater
with a knife no one knew he carried, not even
during the five years he spent at Stateville,
I thought of men and women who sell their blood for
a drink of sleep in a doorway or for a bus ticket
into a night which is also a long drink to nowhere,
and I thought of the blood I was given
when I was nineteen, one transfusion for each year of my life,
and how I promised myself,
if I lived, I would write a poem in honor of blood.
First for my own blood which,
like the letter that begins that alphabet,
is a long cry AAAAH! of relief.
Praise to my own blood which is simple
and accepts almost anything.
And then for the blood that wrestled
all night with my blood
until my veins cramped and the fingers of one hand went rigid.

———

Praise to the blood that wanted to remain alone,
weeping into its own skin,
so that when it flowed into me, my blood contracted
on the knot in its throat. For you
who raised a rash on my arms
and made my body shiver for days, listen,
whoever you are, this poem is for you.

64 Panoramic Way

Like easy conversation,
rambling, obliquely angled,
the winding street traverses
the steep residential hill.

Stone stairs ladder-stitch
the street's tiers; every few
rungs open on terraces,
windows glinting through hedges,

sunlight feathering grass.
At the first switchback,
pine needles tufted with dog fur
pad up the wide cracked steps

leading to a cottage and two
ramshackle shingle houses.
From the lintel of an illegal
basement apartment, magenta

fuchsia, silent bells,
bob and sag over a pot's rim.
Higher, up narrow steps
built over rubble, we climb

to the top deck. What was
our garden now grows wild
onions' white flowers,
and butter-yellow weeds—

winter's mohair throw
draping a bare mattress.
By late spring someone else
or no one will be bending

to pick cool herbs
like single guitar notes.
Something knots in my throat.
Indecipherable

decibels begin jackhammering
inside #D—our old address.
Black Sabbath? Iron Maiden?
I know our own records

by the first chord. Pounding,
we try the unlocked door,
and pick our way through
a year's domestic fall-out:

dropped clothes, album sleeves,
mattresses blocking entrances,
plates, cups, hangers, books.
I trip trying not to look.

Waving on the balcony,
an old guest, now our host,
offers us the view.
At this time of year,

no yellow beach roses
tumble the latticed railing,
no draft of honeysuckle,
no bees flitting near their hive.

Cars nose around the hairpin turn.
Looking past Berkeley's hazy
flat grids, past Oakland,
you can see, as if you've flicked

a painted fan open, a striped
spinnaker tacking the wide bay,
three bridges, and San Francisco
shrugging off her damp negligee.

Carol Muske

Field Trip

Downtown, on the precinct wall,
hangs the map of Gang Territories,
blocks belonging to the red Bloods
or blue Crips. Colored glass hatpins

prick out drive-by death sites—
as the twenty-five five-year-olds
pass by. They hold each other's hands
behind their tour guide, a distracted

man, a sergeant, speaking so far over
their heads, the words snap free
of syntactical gravity: *perpetrator,*
ballistic. The kids freeze in place,

made alert by pure lack of comprehension.
Then, like the dread Med fly, they specialize:
touching fingerprint pads and then their faces,
observing the coffee machine (the plastic cup

that falls and fills in place), the laser printer
burning in the outlines of the Most Wanted
beneath a poster of a skeleton shooting up.
It's not so much that they are literal minds

as minds literally figurative: they inquire
after the skeleton's health. To them a thing
well imagined is as real as what's out the window:
that famous city, city of fame, all trash and high

cheekbones, making itself up with the dreamy paints
of a First Stage Alert. The sergeant can't help
drawing a chalk tree on the blackboard. He wants
them to see that Justice is a metaphor, real as you

and me. Where each branch splits from the trunk,
he draws zeros and says they're fruit, fills each
with a word: arrest, identification, detention,
till sun blinds the slate. Not far away, through

double-thick glass, a young man slumps
on a steel bench mouthing things, a clerk
tallies up personal effects. Now he comes
to the gangs, how they own certain colors

of the prism, indigo, red—he doesn't tell
how they spray-paint neon FUCKs over
the commissioned murals. The kids listen
to the story of the unwitting woman

gunned down for wearing, into the war zone,
a sunset-colored dress. She was mistaken
for herself: someone in red.
She made herself famous, the way people

do here, but unconsciously—becoming
some terrible perfection of style,
bordering as it does, on threat.
The sergeant lifts his ceramic mug,

etched with twin, intertwining hearts,
smiling like a member of a tribe. Later,
on the schoolroom floor, the kids
stretch out, drawing houses with chimneys,

big-headed humans grinning and waving
in lurid, non-toxic crayon. Here is
a policeman, here a crook. Here's a picture
of where I live, my street, my red dress.

Our planet, moon. Our sun.

Little L.A. Villanelle

I drove home that night in the rain.
The gutterless streets filled and overflowed.
After months of drought, the old refrain:

A cheap love song on the radio, off-key pain.
Through the maddening, humble gesture of the wipers,
I drove home that night in the rain.

Hollywood sign, billboard sex: a red stain
spreading over a woman's face, caught mid-scream.
After months of drought, the old refrain.

Marquees on Vine, lit up, name after name,
starring in what eager losses: he dreamed
I drove home that night in the rain.

Smoldering brush, high in the hills. Some inane
preliminary spark: then tiers of falling reflected light.
After months of drought, the old refrain.

I wanted another life, now it drives beside me
on the slick freeway, now it waves, faster, faster—
I drove home that night in the rain.
After months of drought, the old refrain.

Ron Padgett

Poema del City

I live in the city.
It's a tough life,
often unpleasant, sometimes
downright awful. But it has what
we call its compensations.

To kill a roach, for example,
is to my mind not pleasant
but it does develop one's reflexes.
Wham!
and that's that.
Sometimes, though, the battered roach
will haul itself onto broken legs and,
wildly waving its bent antennae,
stagger off into the darkness

to warn the others, who live in the shadow
of the great waterfall in their little teepees.
Behind them rise the gleaming brown and blue mass
of the Grand Tetons, topped with white snow
that blushes, come dawn, and glows, come dusk.
Silent gray wisps rise from the smouldering campfires.

Poema del City 2

A light chill on the knees
& I sneeze
up late, alone, in my house, winter
rain against the window and glittering there
in the constant light from stoops across the street
cars hiss down from one moment to
the next hour: in an hour
I'll be asleep. Wrapped
in new sheets and old quilts
with my wife warm beside me and my son
asleep in the next room, I'll
be so comfortable and dreamy, so happy
I'm not terribly damaged or dying yet
but sailing, secure, secret and all
those other peaceful s's fading
like warm tail lights down a long landscape
with no moon at all.
       Ah, it's sweet,
this living, to make you cry, or rise
& sneeze, and douse the light.

With Lee Remick at Midnight

The lights shoot off the windows of the Plaza
and into the sky where they become stars.

Stars shine over the Playa de Toros
in Mexico, D.F.

We have a Washington, D.C.
We have such a thing as alternating current.

The current flows in one direction for a while
And then in the opposite, alternating rapidly thus.

I get up out of my chair and walk to one end of the room.
There I see a little statue of a friend, Tony Towle.

Hat, coat, muffler and gloves appear on the statue
As the door closes overhead and the sky is black.

My hand reaches for the alarm clock in a dawn
Muddle-headed wha? and I settle into another level

Of being. I want to read Marx, *The Voyage of the Beagle,*
Jean-Jacques Rousseau and Thomas Jefferson, get out

Of bed and meet Bob by noon to have
Mousse au chocolat chez Schrafft's

And be back home in time to hear Fred Flintstone
Give out his mysterious "Yaba-daba-dooo!" wahoo,

As evening settles down in its glorious space
and I shoot down the slide and up, and out

Buffalo

Many times I wait there for my father,
in parking lots of bars or in the bars
themselves, drinking a cherry Coke, Father
joking with a bartender who ignores
him, except to take the orders. I think
of the horrible discipline of bartenders,
and how they must feel to serve, how some shrink
from any conversation to endure
the serving, serving, serving of disease.
I think I would be one of these, eternally
hunched around myself, turning to appease
monosyllabically in the dimness. To flee
enforced darkness in the afternoon
wasn't possible, where was I to go?
Home was too far to walk to, my balloon,
wrinkling in the front seat in the cold, too
awful to go out and play with. Many
times I wait there for Daddy, stupefied
with helpless rage. *Looks old for her age,* any
one of the bartenders said. Outside, the wide
endlessly horizontal vista raged
with sun and snow: it was Buffalo, gleaming
below Great Lakes. Behind bar blinds we were caged,
some motes of sunlight cathedrally beaming.

Animal Mimicry

The sun is setting in another part of the city.
Backlit by a pink bulb slung from an orange cord
Topless Dallas shimmies to her full six feet, palms

Her breasts and gazes into deep space
Before catching her captive audience. Shivering
Once she laughs across the airless airshaft—

"Looks like you're all moved in. Love
The new plants! Lots of, huh, privacy . . ."

Drawing the petalled curtains. Back to
The keyboard—her novel; we unpack more cartons.
Her spaniel's low moan inhabits our bedroom every midnight.

•

Life takes a step forward
Or back.

Box crabs resemble rounded pebbles;
Rocks recall brains.

Beetles identical with rose petals
Adorn a rose bush.

The spots of the Kallima simulate lichens—lichens
Streaked with the knots of the poplars they grow on.

The *Cilax compressa* is confused
With bird droppings.

•

Five weeks here and I move like a native,
A brisk grinding tread that's a Hobson's Choice
Between jail break and death march;

Rear-ending a tourist stalled with his bags
By the intersection of Walk
& Don't Walk, I pitch my body against the traffic—

As if cars and I were equal;
As if all we could do is kill.

Eyes trained on an inner horizon
(But taking everything in, giving nothing back)
I look up into the mirrored

Doorway of the Love Pharmacy to discover
A junkie hawking bird cages—
And myself in a crow black suit

Chattering to myself. Instinctively
I sense I'm home.

•

As a boy snorkeling off Bimini with my Dad

I saw, I swear, black through the sapphire water
An octopus retract its tentacles, curve
Its back, adapt its color, and sink to the floor

A stone . . . Like his cock and balls at the chilly Y
Pool, when we swam nude, withdrawn
to a fluted snail and shell—

No bigger than my own, I shouted,

Until I looked down. Years later in the cancer ward
He asked me to hold him up

While he dripped blood
Into a blue plastic cup.

•

Nights we commune with our fat cat
Elvis, black genius of the new

And old house, his cool ruffled
By sirens, backfirings, screams,

As sightings of the abdicated self-
Exiled sovereign whose name

He bears awaken K-Marts
In Athens and Memphis.

The Chinese, I console him,
Transliterate Elvis

"The King of Cats"—
But still his nerves rasp;

Sleepless, as ten flights down
Another semi shatters Amsterdam,

He mimes a stoic stretch and yawn
(Others he saved,

Himself he could not save)
The next best thing to not being there.

•

Geometer-moths so match shoots of shrubbery
Gardeners cut them with pruning shears;

Phillia browse among themselves,
Taking each other for real leaves.

Startled creatures.

The instinct for self-preservation playing
Leapfrog

With the instinct for renunciation.

•

From a later dinner at the Marlin we returned loaded
To face a short, swaying man and a Doberman he calls My Gun;

Mica in the concrete sets stars winking along the sidewalk,
His acne scars repeat the coarse brick of our building;

A look that translates, it's only money, babes,
And My Gun talking for him at our feet,
I make a show of emptying my wallet;

Yeah, the plastic, he barks, and her purse,
Your watch . . . Those wedding rings,
Keep 'em; I say they always bad luck . . .

Canines grinding, nose high, rearing
On his chain, sniffing,
Gnarling—

Down boy, what you trying to say?
Smart Baby! I think My Gun wants I
Investigate your pockets . . .

You sly dog you, he grins at
Me, while sheepishly I hand over
Twenty-four more dollars.

Look at it like this way,
You buying time;
Place to live—

Till ya met up with My Gun
Again.

Now might we walk you
To your door?

I-guess-you'd-say,
What-can-make-me-feel-this-way?

My Gun, talking 'bout My Gun . . .

You all have nice night.

We see you around.

The Avenues

Some nights when you're off
Painting in your studio above the laundromat,
I get bored about two or three A.M.
And go out walking down one of the avenues
Until I can see along some desolate sidestreet
The glare of an all-night cafeteria.
I sit at the counter,
In front of those glass racks with the long,
Narrow mirrors tilted above them like every
French bedroom you've ever read
About. I stare at all those lonely pies,
Homely wedges lifted
From their moons. The charred crusts and limp
Meringues reflected so shamelessly—
Their shapely fruits and creams all spilling
From the flat pyramids, the isosceles spokes
Of dough. This late at night,
So few souls left
In the place, even the cheesecake
Looks a little blue. With my sour coffee,
I wander back out, past a sullen boy
In leather beneath the whining neon,
Along those streets we used to walk at night,
Those endless shops of spells: the love philtres
And lotions, 20th century voodoo. Once,
Over your bath, I poured
One called *Mystery of the Spies,*
Orange powders sizzling all around your hips.
Tonight, I'll drink alone as these streets haze
To a pale grey. I know you're out somewhere—
Walking the avenues, shadowboxing the rising
Smoke as the trucks leave their alleys and loading
Chutes—looking for breakfast, or a little peace.

David St. John

Uptown Love Poem

I don't mind it so much any more,
All that silver clanging on your ankles
As you step out of your pants,
Grinning; and that tattoo of the mermaid

Along your thigh grows more beautiful
As I slowly rub oil into her scales;
And the sound of your brother's Corvette
Screaming up the avenues is a music

I love to love you by, even in daylight—
Though the white lashes of moonlight on your cheek
Are the reason I was born. And I think I heard
A distant viola on the radio, coming out of

Some window of the building next door,
Or maybe it was just the moan of a dog waking up
On the fire escape, I don't know; but I think
The smell of your skin is the incense

Of the truly sane. I'll take you uptown, where
We can sit all night under a diner's fluorescent
Tongue, all of the waitresses speaking in Spanish
About you, the way your blond hair hangs

Like the Virgin's halo all around your head. Now,
Let's pull the night close slowly, until my face touches
Yours, and the taxis finally quit honking down below—
And the open window slides quietly shut in its swollen,
    sweating frame . . .

Mary Jo Salter

The Rebirth of Venus

He's knelt to fish her face up from the sidewalk
all morning, and at last some shoppers gather
to see it drawn—wide-eyed, and dry as chalk—
whole from the sea of dreams. It's she. None other

than the other one who's copied in the book
he copies from, that woman men divined
ages before a painter let them look
into the eyes their eyes had had in mind.

Love's called him too, today, though she has taught
him in her beauty to love best
the one who first had formed her from a thought.
One square of pavement, like a headstone (lest

anyone mistake where credit lies),
reads BOTTICELLI, but the long-closed dates
suggest, instead, a view of centuries
coming unbracketed, as if the gates

might swing wide to admit, here, in the sun,
one humble man into the pantheon
older and more exalted than her own.
    Slow gods of Art, late into afternoon

let there be light: a few of us drop the wish
into his glinting coinbox like a well,
remembering the forecast. Yet he won't rush
her finish, though it means she'll have no shell

to harbor in; it's clear enough the rain
will swamp her like a tide, and lion-hearted
he'll set off, black umbrella sprung again,
envisioning faces where the streets have parted.

For That Day Only

New York, June 11, 1883

Daybreak, and she left her poppy-seed roll
to follow them as they walked through the city
carrying the dead child, her fourth brother

born in their new world. Sunlight revealed
a stark, unbending man; a hawklike woman
in a stiff wig, wearing a nubby shawl;

and Uncle Ben, with the bouncing silver watch,
their only kin. Now they exhausted sorrow
by humming sacred phrases in the trek

from Allen Street to the Brooklyn cemetery.
Her mother glanced at her, the oldest daughter,
who had rocked beside the stove and read to him

English words that rang like bits of praise
fallen out of prayer, from Homer's tales
of a nymph whose breath filled sails, images

a storyteller scooped out of a basket
that pierced the morning fog, then disappeared,
like a cat's firecoal eyes—alive, but never

as real as asphalt on this long day.
She never saw the film inside his throat,
and had to be pried away when she tried to breathe

life into his mouth. Just before dawn,
she saw their forms as she sang to the baby's pillow;
hands stroked her hand and led her to the march.

And now, how bright they were. How, well—how *visible*.
How steep her father's shoulders. The same light
that warmed them froze gray towers in what was

her first view of the city beyond the neighborhood,
beyond the block. Seeing everything,
trying to see nothing at either side,

she almost smiled at trees, jerked back her head,
remembering herself, and hid her eyes
when she saw a woman speed a bicycle

as though about to rise up over the pavement
like a streetcar's horses that, though ponderous,
might break into a gallop in the wind.

Circles bloomed everywhere: a yellow ball
flew at a hedge; coaches had creaky wheels;
a white hoop, tapped with a stick, zoomed from behind.

There was a brown house with a tulip patch,
for just one family—or so a brass-star
policeman said, who ushered them through crowds

in City Hall Park, and waved at flags on buildings
with plate-glass shop windows. She tripped on loose
cobblestones, and where the streets were roads,

the ground marsh after a night of rain,
she danced and fell, her ankle boots soaked through,
then clambered to the walk and watched a beetle

scurry toward some weeds grown through black gaps
in concrete rectangles. She tried to touch
the statue of a man in bronze that was mottled,

green-going black, with a beckoning,
historical hand, creased at its great wrist.
Longing to stop by a straw-hat cart near a girl

who tugged at a hatless woman with red real hair,
she pushed on to the harbor, where a gull
barely skimmed her head, and climbed the new

Brooklyn Bridge, her alley to the dead.
Chanting lines of the Psalms to secular tunes
that moved her—local streetcries, arias—

she studied the bearded man in front of her,
observed his set jaw, stirred to his praise,
and feared the tiny boy would grow as heavy

as a bag of stones by the time their journey ended.
Stalwart, proud, he held their grief to his chest
for that day only; moments after sunrise

her mother had raised white arms and yielded up
the shapeless sack. Sun growing higher,
she knew that she, the oldest daughter,

would haul that ragged body even after
the procession ended, when they returned
by gaslight to their dim rooms, and, in fact,

whenever she walked alone in her new city,
brick-hard and vast, but never unredeeming,
the next day and the next one and the next.

White Noise

The faces are lifted up into the jumpy light,
the blue electric glow
buzzing them forward into closeup
until the foreground is their eyes, and the fear that is their eyes,
    and tangled hair,
and mouths that grief has torn, clawed open.

(I am lying on a couch in a city that is shadows and glass
and shadows of skyscrapered glass,
that is steel and more steel and billboards
where tall white legs are splayed against white sand, blue surf,
and the red mouths, presiding high above the moving crowds,
are lipsticked, smiling, smooth, and waiting for a cigarette.)

The TV flickers, grays, the faces are gone now
into the undertow
of hunger for the next thing and the next.

(I am lying in a city that is a text unwriting itself,
that is a coffin of glass and a statue of glass,
and the words *why hast thou,* and the words *how many* and *what
    number,*
and *thy Father which is in secret,* and *thy Father
which seeth in secret.)*

And after the news is over the jokes start up,
the studio audience clapping on cue, prerecorded, the theme
    music rising,
the wait right there we'll be back in a minute,
the screen swallowing, swallowing, until there's an anthem,
a test pattern, darkness, and only a pinprick of light breaking
    through.

And somewhere outside of all that are overhead lights and the
    shutting of lights,
there are rows of windows stacked like crates
in the darkness, good night and good night,
and the loneliness that is what's left of the dream of beauty
in which the eyes come back to haunt the empty screen,
the eyes and the hands beneath them
and the mouth saying,

"When I suffer, I cannot forget that I am, nor fail to know
that I am nothing."

Laurie Sheck

The Return

And then he entered the city: in the old stories,
when the hero returns, it is clear where the city begins—
he walks through the arched gateway
cut through the surrounding walls, and he is home.
But now it is more a matter of thinness and thickness:
doorways crowd toward each other like perilous hunched
    shoulders,
windows harden and multiply, vertical and bright.

Here the sky is reddish brown at nightfall
beneath what we still think of as the stars.
Newspapers blow in gutters,
the drained faces of victims and statesmen
press against the pavement, smudged. Or their hands
are lost in the rainbowed oil of passing cars;
the black ink bleeds.

And the people are passing, the crowd of them, so busy,
as if we were still alive—are we alive?
Maybe a questionnaire will lead us to some answer.
It wants to know: How many push-button phones do you have?
Do you use call forward? Have you purchased a phone
within the last six months?

The skyscrapers rise pale green and silver
as if nothing could ever make them burn.
The phones lie in their cradles, sleeping.
I meant to call when I arrived;
is your name still buried in the phone book under "A,"
pressed between the other, similar last names,
laid down there in print deep black as the wires
that carry one human voice to another?

Someone has painted black shadows, human, groping,
eyeless on this alley's dirty walls.
I touch each faceless face, like frost.

Jason Shinder

Prayer

After Jack paces in circles, head down, decides to say
    something to his wife, says nothing,
after Juan no longer eats at the table with his children,
after Gary steals Mrs. Kaufman's six month late welfare check,
after Aaron can no longer lay his head on Esther's breast
    without thinking of Samuel's wife,
after Sy works sixteen hours a day seven days a week one hundred
    and thirty, three hundred, five hundred dollars a week fifty-two
    weeks a year fifty-one years and dies of a heart attack without
    ever really talking to his son, Harold,
after Paulie flickers his knife like a match before young
    Sarie's eyes,
after the Scaletti brothers attack the last no-good hair
    on Louie's head,
after Rudy opens Fred's mouth and blows out his tongue
    with a firecracker,
after Joseph splashes gasoline on his boss's Cadillac,
after watching the drop of sulfur flare up purple-edged
    on the matchstick,
after tossing the match,
after Safiya watches Quincy put Max's hand in a fire and
    waits for the fire to end,
after Pete pounds the girl's head against the sidewalk
    harder than anyone,
after Lucy's father makes her scratch the strange hairs near his groin,
after Harriet leaves her day old child on the steps of
    the movie house,
after Tommy beats his sleepless, irritable son with a baseball bat,
after Chuckie does not break down and confess everything,
after Catherine's moment to confess love passes,
after Fannie's disbelief fans out into clusters of weeds,
after Bobbie is drawn so close to murder it holds her
    before she speaks.

Good Friday. Driving Westward.

. . . being by others hurried every day,
Scarce in a yeare their naturall forme obey:
Pleasure or businesse, so our Soules admit
For their first mover, and are whirld by it.
　　　　　　—John Donne

The rain. Rain that will not end.
The daily errands. Daily bread.
No letting up. No pause
as I steer blindly, circling
the great city. City of tears and blood.
I woke this morning to the ringing phone.
To the last days of the twentieth century.
Hello. Hello. But the line was dead.
The phone in my hand heavy.
My mind whirling. Numb. Taken
against my will closer to oblivion.
At the mall, a man in rags begging
for a coin. My God, only a coin!
I turned my back. Turned back.
But he was gone. Daily, I turn my back.
The suffering of others more and more
like television. Do I drive East? West?
Do I suffer? Shall anger be divine?
Uncorrected, I steer. Swerve
on a slick patch. Lose control.
The rain letting up now. Clouds torn.
The setting sun a brilliant bloody globe.
As if a nailed hand had violently
raked the sky. And then withdrawn.
Past anger or mercy. Leaving me

more distanced. Alone. Driving
this endless road with all the others.
Night and night's Eternity coming on.

The Woman on the Dump

Where was it one first heard the truth? The the.
   —Wallace Stevens

She sits on a smoldering couch
reading labels from old tin cans,
the ground ground down
to dirt, hard as poured cement.
A crowd of fat white gulls
take mincing, oblique steps
around the couch, searching for
an orange rind, a crab claw.
Clouds scud backward overhead,
drop quickly over the horizon,
as if weighted with lead sinkers.
The inside's outside here,
her "sitting room" *en plein air:*
a homey triad of chaise longue,
tilting table, and old floor lamp
from a torn-down whorehouse,
the shade a painted scene
of nymphs in a naked landscape.
The lamp is a beatiful thing,
even if she can't plug it in,
the bare-cheeked, breathless
nymphs part of the eternal
feminine as they rush away
from streaming trees and clouds
that can't be trusted not to change
from man to myth and back again.

The dump's too real. Or not
real enough. It is hot here.
Or cold. When the sun goes down,
she wraps herself in old newspaper,
the newsprint rubbing off,
so that she *is* the news as she
looks for clues and scraps
of things in the refuse. The *the*
is here somewhere, buried
under bulldozed piles of trash.
She picks up a pair of old cymbals
to announce the moon, the pure
symbol, just coming up over there.
Abandoned bathtubs, sinks, and stoves
glow white—abstract forms
in the moonlight—a high tide
of garbage spawns and grows,
throwing long lovely shadows
across unplumbed ravines and gullies.
She'll work through the night,
the woman on the dump,
sifting and sorting and putting
things right, saving everything
that can be saved, rejecting
nothing, piles of tires
in the background unexhaustedly
burning, burning, burning.

Line

Packages under her arm,
a book, it might
rain, it might just
stay cold she thinks
the familiar buildings, steel grey, would ring
if struck and all so perfectly aligned
they move, the crowds surge
like electricity and the bright shop windows
drill into the evening and she breaks
into a run, the bus
is coming and every step is taking
her deeper into the new world.

Our Town

They who had just
put her on the Greyhound bus
leaned on a parked car,
he tapping his fingers
on the roof like they were wondering
what to do with their lives.
A body should be buried
alongside its obsessions:
travel, weather or this
new longing for arrows.
What was never asked for
or had something to fight.
A half a million people
live among the tombstones
of Cairo's largest cemetery.
The setting sun replaces
a few windows in Oakland.
The worlds nobody takes
are inhabited only by hands
and at that, just the palms
in a curved position.

What the City Was Like

The city was full of blue devils,
and, once, during an eclipse, the river
began to glow, and a small body walked out of it
carrying a wooden ship full of vegetables,
which we mistook for pearls.
We made necklaces of them, and tiaras and bracelets,
and the small body laughed until
its head fell off, and soon enough we realized
our mistake, and grew weak with our knowledge.
Across town, a man lived his entire life
without ever going out on the street.
He destroyed his part of the city many times
without getting off his sofa.
But that neighborhood has always blossomed afresh.
Pixies germinated in the still pools under streetlights.
Cattle grazed in back of the bakery
and helped deliver baked goods to the needy.
A mouse issued commands in a benevolent, judicious and
 cheerful manner.
A small, headless body lay in the road,
and passersby clicked their heels.
Across the street the Military Academy
had many historic spots on its windows,
thanks, in part, to the rivers and canals
which carried large quantities of freight
into the treasure-house of maps
and music scores necessary for each war.
The spots were all given names by the janitors—
River of Unwavering Desire, River of Untruth,
Spring of Spies, Rill of Good Enough Hotelkeepers,
and then, of course, there was the Spot of Spots.
Nobody paid any attention to the wars,

though there must have been a few or more.
The citizens of the city were wanderers
who did not live in any one place
but roamed the boulevards and alleyways
picking up gumwrappers and setting them down again.
We were relieved when Modern ice skating
was finally invented: the nuns glided in circles
for days on end, and this was the greatest blessing.
Behind City Hall salt was mined
under a powerful magnifying glass,
and each grain was tasted by someone
named Mildred until she became a stenographer
and moved away, and no one could read
her diacritical remarks, except the little devils.
For years Mildred sent cards at Christmas,
and then nothing, and no one said a thing.
The city was covered with mountains
which ran straight down the center,
and on the southern tip there were several
volcanoes which could erupt on demand.
Or so it was said, though no one demanded proof.
It was a sketchy little volcano of normal girth
where Dolly Madison hosted her parties
more often than I care to remember.
She served ice cream when she was coming.
She came early and stayed late, as they say,
until all the lights were off and the guests
had lost all hope of regaining their senses.
It is not certain if she possessed a cupcake at that time.
She might have had one in her cellar
as no one was allowed to penetrate her there.
And then the prairie dogs arrived
and caused incorrect pips to appear
on the radar screen, for which they became famous,
and which precipitated the rapid decline
of the Know Nothings—not a minute too soon.
In the days that followed children were always screaming.
You could set their hair on fire and, sure enough,
they'd start screaming.

Last Night in Elvisville

Even Memphis smells pretty
Coming out of a tavern:
It's the ghost of Elvis, slinging sachets.
Today was a small one:
At noon, the priests were just waking up with their bells,
And we drank Rock & Roll Beer for breakfast.
Out on the boulevard, I found a hot rock,
Blew on it out of compassion, and
Heard it whisper "No thank you."
But tonight, the sidewalk rushes up to our feet;
A neon light flashes
And we are embarrassed of our expensive lives.
Tomorrow we will, we'll dress them down
And take them to Mississippi to hide in the forest,
Pretending we're simple;
No cop will be able to call us un-American—
Look at our faces:
So eager,
So much wanting whatever we can get.

Lydia Tomkiw

New York Love Song
(Part 1—Lower East Side)

PRELUDE:

Here I am again, doubled over, I'm here, pretending I know what
  I'm doing.
Here again, doubled over in Manhattan dreaming of confetti being
  thrown
For every day is a party, or so I dream; I am dreaming in
  Manhattan.
Here I am in Manhattan, doubled over, dreaming of pretending I
  know what I'm doing in Manhattan.
It is grand.

I
Maybe I should live here, maybe I should know things—
Instead, I hide a blueprint of the streets in my purse.
There is no one here to save me. I must save myself.
I must not get drunk, not on red wine, not on cheap champagne,
Not on the nauseating smell of ghetto palms or burnt pretzels;
I must not get drunk on the street
Vendor's incessant, dead-pan barking of
"Good for cats—made in Poland" and
I must try hard not to look at what he's selling.
I must be able to walk down 3rd street straight and
Make friends with Hell's Angels—
I must be able to make sense of the oriental deli owners' chatter—
They throw me. I must be able to buy flowers, to remember
Where I bought my lottery ticket,
What corner I was grabbed by the shoulders by a homeless

And kissed square on the lips.
I must not get drunk. Maybe I should know things—
Maybe I should live here.
I know I should love here.

II

Near sun-down: 6th street,
Glass chips strung up on a fire escape makes
Mirror ball effect: this city is a cotillion
Where I meet you and meet you and meet you
And we're together forever and ever, again for the very first time.
Give me this forever, give me this and
Summer forever, or at least give me
The memory forever of being
On a roof at night, reclining,
My face facing the heavenly heavens,
Remembering the desperate ride back into Manhattan
In a renegade limo, the city gleaming in front of us like
Some obscene neon fishing lure; and then
Finally flailing into sleep on a chaise longue while
Mobile discos cruised by, blasting Hispanic polkas;
I want to dance; I want to sleep. I want to dance and sleep,
While reclining in my sweat, in the Alphabet Street slumber
    hallucination bed
Floating into the most delicious, panoramic
Dreams of things I can't explain
Because words for them haven't been invented yet—
In any language, I bet.
When I wake up, it's life as unusual.
Everything is embracing me more than I expected.
I like it. It is nice.
I don't know how to make it stay. . . .

David Trinidad

"C'est plus qu'un crime, c'est une faute"

for Amy Gerstler

In the small hours, several rounds
at Le Café, "one of the swankier
spots West L.A.'s nightlife offers":
pink neon and napkins, essence of
scampi and chateaubriand. Seated at
a table against the wall, listen-
ing to the couples on either side
of us chat *en français,* I was
about to comment on the "ambiance"
of the place when, struck by
the looks of a certain redheaded
waiter, you inadvertently spilled
your second strawberry daiquiri.
It seemed everyone turned to
stare at us and you blushed. I'm
afraid I didn't help much, the way
I laughed. I meant to tell you
then, but in the confusion for-
got, how last week, at work, I
found myself attracted to a rather
brawny refrigerator repairman.
He wore a tight white T-shirt,
the tattoo of a chimera half-
visible beneath one of its sleeves.
A chimera is an imaginary monster
made up of incongruous parts. It
is also a frightful or foolish
fancy. I wrote my telephone number

on a small piece of paper and
slipped it in his pocket before
he left. *Why had she acted so
very rashly?* I read this that
night at a drugstore, on the back
cover of a Harlequin Romance, as
I waited in line to buy a pack
of cigarettes. Walking home,
Hollywood Blvd. was abuzz with
tourists and various low-life
types. I reached my street. It
was late, but fireworks were still
being set off from the magicians'
private club at the top of the
hill. I stopped and looked up,
then started to laugh (It had
to be for my benefit!) as half
the night sky briefly flared
into a brilliant shade of red.

Hockney: Blue Pool

Los Angeles,
California:
a summer afternoon.
One boy sunbathes
on a yellow towel
beside the pool;
another stands
at the end of
the diving board,
gazing downward.
Palm trees sway
in the blue water.
Overhead, a few
clouds float by.
To the right,
sprinklers lightly
spray the green
lawn. The sunbather
slips off his red
and white striped
swimsuit and rolls
over; the other
boy dives into the
pool. The artist
snaps a photograph
of the splash.

Carolyne Wright

Return to Seattle: Bastille Day

No difference in the gray gulls, sobbing
like women who circled the tumbrels,
scaffold silhouettes of fir.
The same sky lowers over the channel,

the plane follows it down
like an obsession, guillotine blade
of sun on water. All of this
for what? Walking the green neighborhoods

with names like gracious women: Madrona,
Magnolia. Rain telling its stories
on the ponds, rainbows fracturing
in oil slicks. How could I go back

to where I first took my age
between my hands like a lover's face
and said, "This far, no farther"?
Then moved from one coastline

to the next, as if I had
no winter and no home? For years
it was easy—nothing to answer
for what went beyond the weather,

too soon to give up on the body
or lose myself in the blue
selectivity of dream.
Now, what stands between me

and the long frontier with winter—
A father, sleepwalking among ohms

and voltmeters, the electric smell
of metal. A brother, face-down

in the soft gray light
of the calculus. A sister,
vanished from the glass house
of her thoughts before anyone

could have grown into her name.
My mother, 1945, stepping from
the Armistice Day prop plane
with her unchanged face,

light off the Cascade rain front
troubling her memory with its danger,
years before she could blame
herself for everything.

New York Map Company (1)

Acton Town Manufacturing
Beyond the Bosphorus
Cyprus Minerals
Denver Fire Clay
Eldorado Cleaner
Fresno Touch
Glasgow Botanica
Hanover Hotel
Illinois Bronze Powder and Paint
Jerusalem Cooling
Kitty Hawk Industries
London Towne House
Malta Drydocks
Nottingham Shoes
Osaka Shiatsu Spa
Quincy Compressor
Rio Grande Exchange
Seoul Shoe Repair and Drycleaning
Timbuctoo Timbers
Uranus Sunshine
Venezuela Auto Repair
Warsaw Electric
Xanadu Labs
Yukon Trails Division
Zanzibar Courier Service

Contributors' Notes

Ai's new book, *Greed,* is published by W. W. Norton.

Diane Ackerman is a poet, essayist, and naturalist. She's the author of ten books of poetry and prose, including *Jaguar of Sweet Laughter: New and Selected Poems, A Natural History of the Senses,* and *The Moon by Whale Light.*

Kathleen de Azevedo's poetry has appeared in *Visions International, Sojourner, The Creative Woman, A Fine Madness,* and *The Best American Poetry 1992.* She has poems forthcoming in *Berkeley Poetry Review* and *Owen Wister Review.* She has taught writing and drama to inner city youths in San Francisco.

Judith Baumel's book of poems, *The Weight of Numbers,* won the Walt Whitman Award of the Academy of American Poets. Her poems, essays, and translations have appeared in *The New Yorker, The New York Times Book Review, Poetry, The New Republic,* among many others. She teaches at Adelphi University where she directs the creative writing program.

Lucie Brock-Broido is the author of *A Hunger* (Knopf, 1988). Her second collection, *The Master Letters,* is forthcoming from Knopf. She is an Associate Professor in Poetry at Columbia University.

Marilyn Chin was born in Hong Kong and raised on the West Coast. Her first book, *Dwarf Bamboo* (Greenfield Review Press, 1987), was nominated for the Bay Area Book Reviewers Award. The poems in this anthology will appear in her second book, *The*

211

Phoenix Gone, the Terrace Empty (Milkweed Editions, 1994). She teaches in the MFA program at San Diego State University.

Amy Clampitt was born and brought up in rural Iowa, graduated from Grinnell College, and has since lived mainly in New York City. She is the author of five collections of poetry; the latest, *A Silence Opens*, was published in February 1994.

Elizabeth Cohen's poems and stories have appeared in *Poet Lore, Kalliope, Ellipsis*, and other magazines. Her chapbook of poems, *Impossible Furniture*, was published in 1993 by Nightshade Press. Currently the president of Poetlink/The Poetry Launderette, a Brooklyn organization that sponsors a poetry reading and workshop series, she works as an editorial assistant at *The New York Times*.

Thulani Davis is the author of two books of poetry, *Playing the Changes* and *All the Renegade Ghosts Rise*, as well as the libretto for the acclaimed opera *X, The Life and Times of Malcolm X*, by Anthony Davis. Her most recent books are *1959*, a novel, and *Malcolm X, The Great Photographs*.

Connie Deanovich is a recipient of the GE Award for Younger Writers, and has been anthologized in *Under 35: The New Generation of American Poets* and published in *New American Writing, Sulfur*, and elsewhere. She is the editor of *B City*. Her chapbook, *Ballerina Criminology*, was published by Pink Dog Press, Toronto.

Tom Disch's seventh collection of poems, *Dark Verses and Light*, was published by Johns Hopkins University Press in 1991. His most recent novel, *The Priest: A Gothic Romance* (Knopf), is the third in a series that includes *The Businessman: A Tale of Terror* and *The M.D.: A Horror Story*.

Mark Doty's *Turtle, Swan* and *Bethlehem in Broad Daylight* were published by David R. Godine; *My Alexandria* was chosen for the National Poetry Series by Philip Levine and published by the University of Illinois Press in 1993. He teaches at Sarah Lawrence College and at the Vermont College MFA program.

Rita Dove is the Poet Laureate of the United States for 1993–94. She received the 1987 Pulitzer Prize for her third book of poems, *Thomas and Beulah;* other poetry books include *The Yellow House on the Corner, Museum, Grace Notes* (Norton), and most recently *Selected Poems* (Vintage, 1993). Ms. Dove teaches creative writing at the University of Virginia.

Cornelius Eady is the author of three books of poetry, *Kartunes, Victims of the Latest Dance Craze,* winner of the 1985 Lamont Prize from the American Academy of Poets, and *The Gathering of My Name.* He is currently Assistant Professor of English and Director of The Poetry Center at SUNY Stony Brook.

Barbara Elovic lives in Booklyn, New York. Her poems have appeared in many journals, including *Poetry, MSS, Passages North,* and *The Threepenny Review.* She's also had work included in the *Anthology of Magazine Verse* and *Waltzing on Water,* an anthology for young adults.

Lynn Emanuel is the author of two books of poetry, *Hotel Fiesta* (University of Georgia) and *The Dig* (University of Illinois). She has been recognized by two NEA Fellowships, the National Poetry Series, and the Great Lakes Colleges Association's New Writers Award. Currently, she is an Associate Professor at the University of Pittsburgh.

Elaine Equi is the author of six collections of poetry including, most recently, *Surface Tension,* published by Coffee House Press. A new book, *Decoy*, is forthcoming in 1993 from The Figures Press. She currently lives in New York City and teaches workshops at The New School and The Writer's Voice.

Martín Espada was awarded both the PEN/Revson Fellowship and the Paterson Poetry Prize for his third book, *Rebellion Is the Circle of a Lover's Hands* (Curbstone Press, 1990). His most recent collection, *City of Coughing and Dead Radiators*, was published by Norton in 1993.

Alice Fulton's books include *Powers of Congress* (David R. Godine), *Palladium* (University of Illinois), and *Dance Script with Electric Ballerina* (University of Pennsylvania). In 1991, she was awarded a MacArthur Fellowship. She's Professor of English at The University of Michigan, Ann Arbor.

Amy Gerstler is a writer of fiction and poetry living in Los Angeles. Her book, *Bitter Angel*, won a National Book Critics' Circle Award in poetry in 1991. In November 1993, Viking Penguin published a collection of her poems entitled *Nerve Storm*.

Debora Greger is the author of four books of poetry: *Movable Islands* (1980), *And* (1986), *The 1002nd Night* (Princeton University Press, 1990), and *Off-Season at the Edge of the World* (University of Illinois Press, 1994). She teaches in the creative writing program at the University of Florida.

Linda Gregg's new book, *Chosen by the Lion*, will be published by Graywolf in the spring of 1994. Her current book, *The Sacraments of Desire*, is now out in paperback. Her first two books will be reprinted by Graywolf next year as well.

Jessica Hagedorn is the author of the novel *Dogeaters* (nominated for the National Book Award in the fiction category) and the collection of poetry and prose *Danger and Beauty*, both available in paperback from Penguin Books. She is also the editor of *Charlie Chan Is Dead: An Anthology of Contemporary Asian American Fiction* (Viking Penguin, 1993), and is writing a second novel.

Edward Hirsch has published four books of poems: *For the Sleepwalkers* (1981), *Wild Gratitude* (1986), *The Night Parade* (1989), and *Earthly Measures* (1994). He teaches at the University of Houston.

Garrett Hongo was born in Volcano, Hawaii, in 1951. He is the author of *Yellow Light* (Wesleyan, 1982) and *The River of Heaven* (Knopf, 1988), which was the Lamont Poetry Selection of the Academy of American Poets in 1987. He recently edited *The Open Boat: Poems from Asian America* (Anchor, 1993). He is currently Professor of Creative Writing at the University of Oregon.

Richard Howard's tenth book of poems, *Like Most Revelations*, was published in March 1994, by Pantheon. A winner of the Pulitzer Prize for Poetry, he is also a critic and translator, and a Professor of English at the University of Houston.

Lynda Hull is the author of two collections of poetry, *Ghost Money*, the 1986 Juniper Prize winner, and *Star Ledger*, which was published in 1991 by University of Iowa Press. She was born in 1954 in Newark, New Jersey, and presently lives in Chicago. She teaches at the Vermont College MFA Program.

Esther Iverem's first book of poems and photographs, *The Time: Portrait of a Journey Home*, was published in 1993 by Africa World Press. Her articles, essays, and poems have been published widely. She is a graduate of the University of Southern California and Columbia University. A native of Philadephia, she now lives in New York City with her husband, the writer Nick Chiles, and her baby boy, Mazi.

Mark Jarman grew up in greater Los Angeles. He is the author of *Iris*, a book-length poem, and *The Black Riviera*, winner of the 1991 Poets' Prize, among other books. He teaches at Vanderbilt University.

Patricia Spears Jones, a native of Arkansas, has lived in the Northeast—mostly New York City—for twenty years. She is author of *Key of Permanent Blue* and coeditor of *Ordinary Women: New York City Women Poets*. Her work is anthologized in *Black Sister* and *Home Girls*. She was recently commissioned to write the text for a new theater work by the experimental theater company Mabou Mines.

Rodney Jones, the author of *The Story They Told Us of Light*, *The Unborn*, *Transparent Gestures*, and *Apocalyptic Narrative and Other Poems*, teaches at Southern Illinois University at Carbondale. Recipient of awards from the Academy of American Poets and the American Academy and Institute of Arts and Letters, he won the 1989 National Book Critics Circle Award for *Transparent Gestures*.

Lawrence Joseph was born in Detroit, Michigan, in 1948. His books of poems are *Shouting at No One* (1983), which received the Starrett Poetry Prize, and *Curriculum Vitae* (1988), both published in the Pitt Poetry Series. His third book, *Before Our Eyes*, was published in 1993 by Farrar, Straus & Giroux. He presently is Professor of Law at St. John's University School of Law.

Vickie Karp is a senior writer for public television and former assistant poetry editor at *The New Yorker*. Her work includes the documentary film *Marianne Moore: In Her Own Image*, the play *Driving to the Interior*, and poems published in *The New Yorker*, *The New York Review of Books*, *The New Republic*, and *The Yale Review*.

Karl Kirchwey is the author of two books of poems, *Those I Guard* (1993) and *A Wandering Island* (1990). He is the recipient of the Norma Farber First Book Award of the Poetry Society of America, and in 1993 was awarded an Ingram Merrill Foundation Fellowship. Karl Kirchwey is Director of the Unterberg Poetry Center of the 92d Street YM-YWHA in New York.

August Kleinzahler is the author of *Storm Over Hackensack* and *Earthquake Weather*. He is a recipient of fellowships from the General Electric Foundation, the Guggenheim Foundation, and the Lila Wallace–Reader's Digest Fund. He lives in San Francisco.

Yusef Komunyakaa is currently Professor of English and African-American Studies at Indiana University and was the 1992 Holloway Lecturer at the University of California at Berkeley. His latest books are *Magic City* and *Neon Vernacular: New and Selected Poems*. He is also coeditor (with Sascha Feinstein) of *The Jazz Poetry Anthology*.

David Lehman's most recent book of poems is *Operation Memory* (Princeton University Press, 1990). He is also the author of several nonfiction books, including *Signs of the Times: Deconstruction and the Fall of Paul de Man*. He won a three-year Writer's Award from the Lila Wallace–Reader's Digest Fund in 1991.

Philip Levine was born and raised in Detroit, went to college at Wayne State University, and found poetry first in Detroit. Later found it in New York City, Barcelona, and Fresno.

Dionisio D. Martínez, born in Cuba, is the author of *History as a Second Language* (Ohio State University Press/*The Journal* Poetry Award) and *Dancing at the Chelsea* (State Street Press). The recipient of a Whiting Award for 1993, he will publish his third book, *Bad Alchemy*, with Norton.

Donna Masini's poems have appeared in *The Paris Review, Georgia Review, Boulevard, Parnassus, Pequod,* et al. She was a 1991 recipient of an NEA fellowship. Her book of poems, *That Kind of Danger,* was selected by Mona Van Duyn for the 1993 Barnard Woman Poet's Prize and published by Beacon Press. She has always lived in New York City.

Robert Mazzocco: Poet and critic; longtime contributor to *The New Yorker* and *The New York Review of Books;* published *Trader* in 1980; essays and poems reprinted in various anthologies; traveled widely throughout the Americas; has lived abroad in Europe, Asia, and the South Seas.

Susan Mitchell is the author of two books of poems, *Rapture* (HarperCollins, 1992) and *The Water Inside the Water* (Wesleyan, 1983). She received the Guggenheim and Lannan literary fellowships in 1992 and the Kingsley Tufts Poetry Award for *Rapture* in 1993. She has been the Mary Blossom Lee Professor in Creative Writing at Florida Atlantic University in Boca Raton since 1987.

Carol Moldaw's first book of poems, *Taken from the River,* was published by Alef Books in 1993. Her poems have appeared in *The New Yorker, The New Republic, Kenyon Review, Agni Review,* and other journals, as well as *Under 35: The New Generation of American Poets.* She lives in Pojoaque, New Mexico.

Carol Muske is a professor at USC and author of five books of poems and two novels (most recently *Red Trousseau* and *Saving St. Germ* from Viking). She's won several awards, including a Guggenheim and an NEA, and reviews regularly for *The New York Times Book Review.* She lives in L.A. with her husband, actor David Dukes, and their daughter, Annie.

Ron Padgett's books include *Great Balls of Fire, Toujours l'amour, Tulsa Kid, Triangles in the Afternoon, The Big Something,* and *Blood Work: Selected Prose.* His most recent translation is *The Complete Poems of Blaise Cendrars.* A recipient of Guggenheim and National Endowment for the Arts fellowships, Padgett lives in New York City.

Molly Peacock, President of the Poetry Society of America, is the author of three books of poems: *And Live Apart, Raw Heaven,* and *Take Heart.* In 1993 she was Poet-in-Residence at Bucknell University. Originally from Buffalo, the Queen City, she now lives in New York City and in London, Ontario, the Forest City.

Robert Polito was born in Boston. He will publish two books in 1994, *A Reader's Guide to James Merrill's 'The Changing Light at Sandover'* (University of Michigan Press) and *Savage Art: A Life of Jim Thompson* (Knopf). He lives in New York City, where he directs the Writing Program at the New School for Social Research.

David St. John is the author of *Hush, The Shore, No Heaven,* and *Terraces of Rain: An Italian Sketchbook.* His most recent volume is *Study for the World's Body: New and Selected Poems* (1994), published by HarperCollins. He is Poetry Editor of *The Antioch Review.*

Mary Jo Salter was born in Grand Rapids, Michigan, and was educated at Harvard and at Cambridge. Her three books of poems, *Henry Purcell in Japan* (1985), *Unfinished Painting* (1989), winner of the Lamont Prize, and *Sunday Skaters* (1994), are published by Knopf. She is Poetry Editor of *The New Republic.*

Grace Schulman's newest poetry collection, *For That Day Only,* will be published by Sheep Meadow Press in September 1994. Her past books of poems include *Burn Down the Icons* and *Hemispheres.* Author of *Marianne Moore: The Poetry of Engagement,* Schulman is

Poetry Editor of *The Nation* and a Professor of English at Baruch College, CUNY.

Laurie Sheck was born in the Bronx, New York. Her most recent book of poems is *Io at Night* (Knopf). She was a Guggenheim Fellow in Poetry for 1991, and currently teaches at Rutgers University.

Jason Shinder is the author of the poetry collection *Every Room We Ever Slept In* (Sheep Meadow Press, 1993), and the editor of the anthologies *Divided Light: Father and Son Poems* (Sheep Meadow Press), *First Light: Mother and Son Poems*, and *More Light: Father and Daughter Poems* (Harcourt Brace). His forthcoming books include the novel *Liars* and the anthologies *Screen Gems: Movie Poems* and *Eternal Light: Grandparent Poems*.

Elizabeth Spires is the author of three books of poetry: *Globe* (Wesleyan, 1981), *Swan's Island* (Holt, 1985), and *Annonciade* (Viking/Penguin, 1989). A recipient of fellowships from the Guggenheim Foundation and the National Endowment for the Arts, she lives in Baltimore and teaches at Goucher College and in the Writing Seminars at Johns Hopkins University.

Cole Swensen's recent books include *Park* (Floating Island Publications, 1991) and *New Math* (William Morrow and Company, 1988). Her work has also appeared in the anthologies *Under 35: The New Generation of American Poets* (Anchor, 1989), *Waltzing on Water* (Dell, 1989), and *How the Net Is Gripped* (Stride Publications, 1992). Her translations of contemporary French and Russian poets have appeared in a variety of journals.

James Tate's *Selected Poems*, published in 1991, received the Pulitzer Prize and the William Carlos Williams Award. His first book, *The Lost Pilot*, won the Yale Series of Younger Poets Award in 1967.

Other books include: *The Oblivion Ha-Ha* (1970), *Hints to Pilgrims* (1971), *Absences* (1972), *Viper Jazz* (1976), *Riven Doggeries* (1979), *Constant Defender* (1983), *Reckoner* (1986), and *Distance from Loved Ones* (1990).

Lydia Tomkiw's collections include *The Dreadful Swimmers* (Wide Skirt, England), *A Redhead in Trouble, Stellazine, Thank You,* among others. Her work has appeared in many publications both in the U.S. and abroad. She performs with the poetry/music group, Algebra Suicide, which has released nine full-length albums, and tours internationally.

David Trinidad's collections include *Monday, Monday* (1985), *November* (1987), and *Hand Over Heart: Poems 1981–1988* (1991). His poetry has appeared in numerous magazines and anthologies, including *Harper's, The Paris Review, Mondo Barbie, High Risk,* and *The Best American Poetry 1991.* Originally from Los Angeles, Trinidad now lives in New York City.

Carolyne Wright grew up in Seattle. She has published two books and two chapbooks of poetry, and translated *In Order to Talk with the Dead: Selected Poems of Jorge Teillier* (University of Texas Press, 1993). She is completing a two-volume anthology of her translations of Bengali women poets and writers. Now living near Boston, she teaches in the Summer School Writing Program at Harvard University.

John Yau is a poet, fiction writer, critic, and curator. He is the author of sixteen books of poetry, most recently *Edificio Sayonara* (Black Sparrow, 1992). In 1992, he and Bill Barrette received the Brendan Gill Prize for their collaboration of poems and photographs, *Big City Primer: Reading New York City at the End of the Twentieth Century* (Timken Publishers, 1991). He lives in New York City.